Footprint Handbook
# Seville

NDY SYMINGTON

# This is
Seville

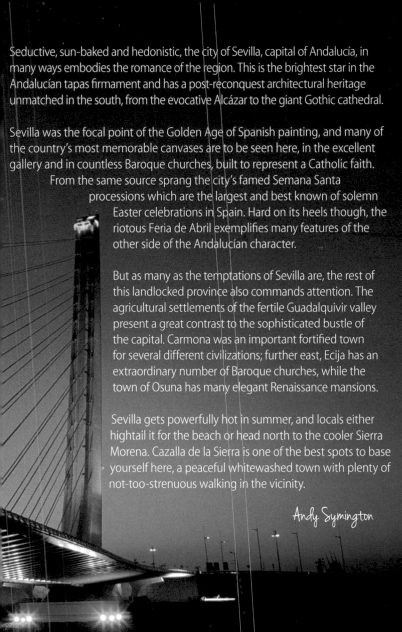

Seductive, sun-baked and hedonistic, the city of Sevilla, capital of Andalucía, in many ways embodies the romance of the region. This is the brightest star in the Andalucían tapas firmament and has a post-reconquest architectural heritage unmatched in the south, from the evocative Alcázar to the giant Gothic cathedral.

Sevilla was the focal point of the Golden Age of Spanish painting, and many of the country's most memorable canvases are to be seen here, in the excellent gallery and in countless Baroque churches, built to represent a Catholic faith. From the same source sprang the city's famed Semana Santa processions which are the largest and best known of solemn Easter celebrations in Spain. Hard on its heels though, the riotous Feria de Abril exemplifies many features of the other side of the Andalucían character.

But as many as the temptations of Sevilla are, the rest of this landlocked province also commands attention. The agricultural settlements of the fertile Guadalquivir valley present a great contrast to the sophisticated bustle of the capital. Carmona was an important fortified town for several different civilizations; further east, Ecija has an extraordinary number of Baroque churches, while the town of Osuna has many elegant Renaissance mansions.

Sevilla gets powerfully hot in summer, and locals either hightail it for the beach or head north to the cooler Sierra Morena. Cazalla de la Sierra is one of the best spots to base yourself here, a peaceful whitewashed town with plenty of not-too-strenuous walking in the vicinity.

Andy Symington

# Best of
# Seville

## ❶ Cathedral, Sevilla city

Sevilla's cathedral is a marvellous Gothic edifice on a monumental scale that imposes by its sheer bulk. Its numerous side chapels are a wonderful repository of art, while its Moorish tower, the Giralda, and the weather vane atop it are famous city landmarks. Page 11.

## ❷ Real Alcázar, Sevilla city

Built after the Reconquest but in Moorish style, this handsome palace and fortress of the kings of Castile recalls the glories of the period with a series of handsome chambers featuring beautifully detailed stucco work, calligraphy and arches, and a sumptuous walled garden. Page 15.

## ❸ Parque María Luisa, Sevilla city

The 1929 Ibero-American Exhibition was held here and left a legacy in a series of striking buildings centred around the enticing Parque María Luisa. Particularly notable is the huge semicircle of the Plaza de España, the upmarket Alfonso XIII hotel and the city's archaeological museum. Page 25.

## 6 Casa de Pilatos, Sevilla city

This ducal mansion on the edge of atmospheric Barrio Santa Cruz is one of Sevilla's most impressive aristocratic homes. A blend of Renaissance and *mudéjar* architecture, it has an elegantly classical feel and a stunning central courtyard. Page 31.

## 4 Triana and La Macarena, Sevilla city

These working-class barrios are redolent with the essence and mystique of Sevilla, and make fantastic places for a stroll. Reverence for Semana Santa sculptures, flamenco, local character in markets and workshops and a palpable sense of tradition and history make these places special. Pages 28 and 33.

## 5 El Ayuntamiento, Sevilla city

Sevilla's town hall is set between two plazas in the heart of town. It was built in two distinct phases and features some stunning Renaissance stonework. It's well worthwhile taking the guided tour of its interior to appreciate the impressive carved function rooms. Page 31.

## 7 Museo de Bellas Artes, Sevilla city

The city's main art gallery has a wonderful collection of Spanish painting in a characterful former monastery. Local boy Velázquez is represented, but the gallery is particularly notable for its brilliant works by the giants of Sevilla's Golden Age of art: Zurbarán and Murillo. Page 32.

EXTREMADURA

LA MACARENA ④

**Río Guadalquivir**
Torneo

Alfonso XII
⑦ 🏛 Museo de Bellas Artes

Casa de Pilatos
⑤ ⑥

☐ Ayuntamiento

Paseo Cristóbal Colón

① ✝ Cathedral

Real
Alcázar
②

④
TRIANA

Menéndez Pelayo

③ Parque
María
Luisa

Sierra

Sierra Morena

◇ Guadalcanal

Alanís
⑨

♦ Parque Natural
Sierra Norte

Cazalla de
la Sierra

Constantina

El Pedroso

A432

Peñaflor

Lora
del Río

N431

A45

Cantillana

A436

A66
N630

Gerena

Aznalcóllar

Guillena

HUELVA

⑧
Italica

A472

Carmona
⑩

A4

SEVILLA

Sevilla ✈

Alcalá de
Guadaira

A398

A49

A443

A4

A472

Coria

A4

Villafranco del
Guadalquivir

NIV

Dos Hermanas

A92

A376

Arahal

Marchena

A92

Osuna

Las Palacios
y Villafranca

A394

A361

Utrera

Parque Natural
Brazo del Este

♦ Parque Nacional
Coto Doñana

Morón de
la Frontera

El Palmar
de Troya

A375

Villanueva
de San Juan

Las Cabezas
de San Juan

A8126

Lebrija

A384

A471

NIV

A4

Olvera

A393

CADIZ

Sanlúcar de
Barrameda

Arcos de
la Frontera

A374

Jerez de la
Frontera

N

Ronda

Ubrique

10 km
10 miles

## ⑧ Itálica

Wander the ruins of what was once one of the Roman Empire's largest cities, a large complex that was originally built as a rest-and-relaxation base for troops. It's easily accessed on local buses from Sevilla and can be combined with a visit to an interesting nearby monastery. Page 36.

## ⑨ Sierra Morena

The wooded hills of the northern part of Sevilla province can come as a cool relief after the baking heat of its central plains. Cazalla de la Sierra is the best base for exploration, a whitewashed town that offers walking trails and local liqueurs. Page 53.

## ⑩ Carmona

Atmospheric Carmona is an easy day trip from Sevilla and offers a pleasantly compact old centre, ideal for strolling. The highlight is the Roman necropolis: descending into its enormous patrician tombs is a thrill; some of them preserve wall paintings. Page 55.

# Sevilla city

The capital of Andalucía was accurately described in the 16th century as having 'the smell of a city and of something undefinable, of another greatness'. While the fortunes of this one-time mercantile powerhouse have waxed and waned, its allure has not; even within Spain its name is spoken like a mantra, a word laden with sensuality and promise. Delving beyond the famous icons; the horse carriages, the oranges, the flamenco, the haunting Semana Santa celebrations, you find a place where being seen is nothing unless you're seen to be having fun, a place where the ghosts of Spain walk the streets, be they fictional, like Don Juan or Carmen, or historical, like Cervantes, Columbus, Caesar or Joselito.

Sevilla has an astonishingly rich architectural heritage within its enormous old town, still girt by sections of what was once Europe's longest city wall. The bristling Moorish tower of the Torre del Oro, the Baroque magnificence of numerous churches; the gigantic Gothic cathedral and the *mudéjar* splendours of the Alcázar; these and much more are ample reason to spend plenty of time in Sevilla; you could spend weeks here and not get to see all the sights.

But the supreme joy of the city is its tapas. They claim to have invented them here, and they are unbeatable; you'll surely find that your most pleasurable moments in this hot, hedonistic city come with glass and fork in hand.

# Essential Sevilla city

## Getting around

Most sights are in the old town. As it was once one of the biggest cities in Europe, this is a fairly large area. However, much of it are pedestrianized and walking is by far the best way to get around.

### Bus

To avoid the fierce summer heat, take one of Sevilla's air-conditioned city buses. Bus C5 does a useful circuit around the centre, including La Macarena.

## Best tapas bars

**Ovejas Negras**, page 42
**Bar Alfalfa**, page 43
**Bodega Santa Cruz**, page 43
**Casa Morales**, page 44
**Yebra**, page 45

### Metro

Sevilla has a metro, www.metro-sevilla.es, with only one line operational until at least 2017. Line 1 links the satellite towns of Mairena de Aljarafe and Dos Hermanas with the centre. Useful stops are Prado de San Sebastián bus station, Puerta de Jerez near the cathedral and Barrio Santa Cruz, Plaza de Cuba at one end of Triana, Parque de los Príncipes in Los Remedios, and Nervión, the prime modern shopping area near Sevilla football stadium. However, most of the interesting parts of tourist Sevilla are not covered by the network. A single costs €1.35 for short journeys.

### Taxi

Taxis are a good way to get around. A green light on means they are available and they are comparatively cheap.

### Tram

Sevilla has a tram service. Line 1 of Metrocentro handily zips between Plaza Nueva and San Bernardo local train station, via the cathedral, Puerta de Jerez and the Prado de San Sebastián bus station. A single ticket costs €1.40.

## When to go

Peak season, when prices are notably higher, in Sevilla is March to May, with the most pleasant weather and the two major festivals, Semana Santa and Feria de Abril. Summer is a quiet time as temperatures can be almost unbearable (hitting 50°C in recent years); autumn is a good time to visit, and winter is much milder here than elsewhere in Europe.

## Time required

At least three days to see the main sights.

## Weather Sevilla

| January | February | March | April | May | June |
|---|---|---|---|---|---|
| 15°C 6°C 73mm | 17°C 6°C 59mm | 20°C 9°C 38mm | 23°C 11°C 51mm | 26°C 13°C 36mm | 32°C 17°C 9mm |

| July | August | September | October | November | December |
|---|---|---|---|---|---|
| 36°C 20°C 1mm | 36°C 20°C 5mm | 32°C 18°C 25mm | 26°C 14°C 60mm | 20°C 10°C 84mm | 16°C 7°C 95mm |

vast Gothic cathedral and sumptuous *mudéjar* Alcázar

*Plaza del Triunfo s/n, T954-214971, www.catedraldesevilla.es. Mon 1100-1530, Tue-Sat 1100-1700, Sun 1430-1800, you can prebook a free visit including audioguide on Mon 1630-1800. €8/€4 students under 26 and retirees. You can buy tickets online to avoid queues.*

★Sevilla's bases of ecclesiastical and royal power, the cathedral and Alcázar face each other across the sun-beaten Plaza del Triunfo, once just inside the city's major gateway. They're both heavily visited, and with good reason: you should give plenty of your time to visit either and linger in a quiet corner while the tourist groups surge past. In the squares around, horse carriages sit under the orange trees ready to trot visitors around the sights of the town.

The fall of Sevilla to the Christians in 1248 was an event of massive resonance. While Granada's capitulation in 1492 marked the final victory, it was something of a foregone conclusion – the fall of Sevilla really represented the breaking of the backbone of Muslim Spain. After a while, at the beginning of the 15th century, the Castillians decided to hammer home the point and erect a cathedral over the mosque (which they had been using as a church), on a scale that would leave no doubts.

Santa María de la Sede is the result, which contains so many riches that most of its chapels and altars could have been tourist attractions in their own right; there are nearly 50 of them.

Several Moorish elements were happily left standing; the city's symbol, the superb Giralda tower, is the most obvious of these. Originally the minaret of the mosque, it was built by the Almohads in the late 12th century and was one of the tallest buildings in the world in its day. Although rebuilt by the Christians after its destruction in an earthquake, its emblematic exterior brick decoration is true to the original, although the famous weather vane atop the structure (El Giraldillo) is not.

Approaching the cathedral, try and start from Plaza de San Francisco, behind the Ayuntamiento. Taking Calle Hernando Colón, another Moorish feature will soon become apparent – the Puerta del Perdón gateway, with fine stucco decoration and a dog-toothed horseshoe arch. Turning left and walking around the whole structure will let you appreciate the Giralda and the many fine 15th-century Gothic doorways. You enter via the soaring Puerta San Cristóbal, next to the Archivo de las Indias.

It's impossible to list here all the works of artistic merit contained within the huge five-naved space. After passing through the entrance the first chamber is a small museum with several excellent pieces including a head of the Baptist by Juan de Mesa; a Roldán Joseph and Child; a San Fernando by Murillo; and a Zurbarán depicting the Baptist in the desert.

### Around the chapels
Once into the cathedral proper, after catching your breath at the dimensions and the pillars like trunks of an ancient stone forest, turn hard left and do a circuit of

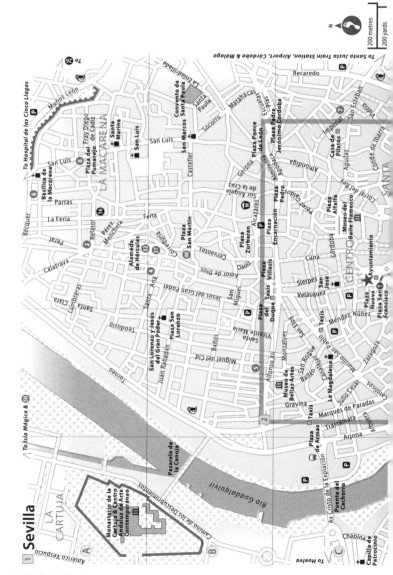

# Sevilla

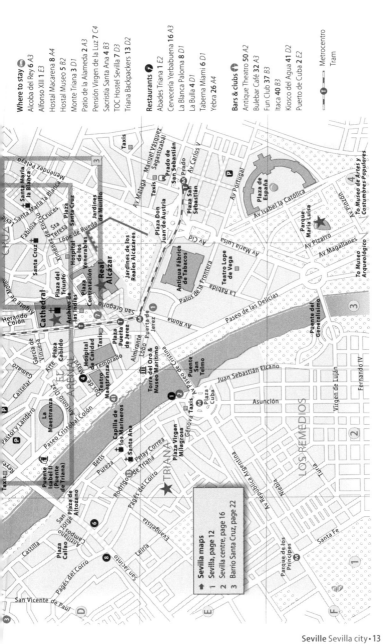

## Where to stay

Alcoba del Rey **6** A3
Alfonso XIII **1** E3
Hostal Macarena **8** A4
Hostal Museo **5** B2
Monte Triana **3** D1
Patio de la Alameda **2** A3
Pensión Virgen de la Luz **7** C4
Sacristía Santa Ana **4** B3
TOC Hostel Sevilla **7** D3
Triana Backpackers **13** D2

## Restaurants

Abades Triana **1** E2
Cervecería Yerbabuena **16** A3
La Blanca Paloma **8** D1
La Bulla **4** D1
Taberna Miami **6** D1
Yebra **26** A4

## Bars & clubs

Antique Theatro **50** A2
Bulebar Café **32** A3
Fun Club **37** B3
Itaca **40** B3
Kiosco del Agua **41** D2
Puerto de Cuba **2** E2

━━━ Metrocentro
Tram

**Sevilla maps**
1 Sevilla, page 12
2 Sevilla centre, page 16
3 Barrio Santa Cruz, page 22

the chapels. Don't forget to look up once in a while to appreciate the lofty Gothic grandeur and the excellent stained glass, much of it by Heinrich of Germany (15th century) and Arnao of Flanders (16th century). At the western end of the church, Murillo's *Guardian Angel* stands to the left of the middle door, leading the Christ child by the hand.

Turning on to the north side, see if you can barge through the tour groups into the chapel of **San Antonio**, with a huge and much-admired Murillo of that saint's vision of a cloud of cherubs and angels. Above it is a smaller Baptism by the same artist. An impressive Renaissance baptismal font here is still in use, while a 15th-century frieze of saints adorns the *reja*. These *rejas* are works of art in their own right – some of them take wrought iron to extraordinary delicacy.

Arriving in the northeast corner, take a break from chapels and climb the **Giralda**. You reach the top via 35 ramps (if they weren't numbered you'd think you were in a neverending Escher sketch), designed to allow sentries to climb the tower on horseback. The tower is 94 m high and the view from the top is excellent and helps to orientate yourself in this confusing city. There's a host of bells up here; the oldest date from the 14th century.

Coming down, the next chapel of **San Pedro** contains a *retablo* with nine good Zurbaráns devoted to the first pope's life. The inspiring **Royal Chapel** is often curtained off for services. The cuissons of its masterly domed ceiling contain busts of Castilla's kings and queens. In a funerary urn are the remains of the sainted conqueror-king Fernando III, while his wife Beatrice of Swabia (the inspiration behind Burgos cathedral) and their son Alfonso X (the Wise) are also buried here.

In the southeast corner, the treasury is entered through the **Mariscal Chapel**, which has a stunning altarpiece centred on the Purification of Mary and painted by Pedro de Campaña (Pieter Kempeneer), a Fleming of exalted talent. The **Treasury** contains a display of monstrances (one of which holds a spine from the Crown of Thorns), salvers and processional crowns. A fine antechamber and courtyard adjoin the Chapterhouse, adorned with vault paintings by Murillo.

The massive vestry is almost a church in its own right, with an ornate Plateresque entrance and three altars featuring fine paintings; a moving Descent from the Cross by Pedro de Campaña, a Santa Teresa by Zurbarán and a San Laurencio by Jordán. Two Murillos face each other across the room; they depict two of the city's earliest archbishops from the Visigothic period, San Isidoro and San Leandro.

Columbus' tomb stands proud in the southern central doorway, borne aloft by four figures representing the kingdoms of Castilla, León, Aragón and Navarra. It's in late 19th-century Romantic style, and some remains were deposited there in 1902, but nobody knows for sure whose they are – Sevilla is one of four cities that claim to have the fair-dinkum Columbus tomb. Columbus spent time praying in the next chapel, which features an excellent 14th-century fresco of Mary, in the place where the mosque's *mihrab* once stood. The later *retablo* was built around the painting.

The cathedral's principal devotional spaces are in the centre of the massive five-naved structure – the choir and the chancel. The choir itself is closed off by a noteworthy gilt Plateresque *reja* depicting the Tree of Jesse, while the ornate stalls feature misericords with charismatic depictions of demons and the vices.

The main *retablo* is a marvel of Christian art and has been the subject of several books in its own right. Measuring a gigantic 18 m by 28 m, it was masterminded by the Fleming Pieter Dancart, who began it in 1481; several other notable painters and sculptors worked on it until its completion in 1526. It is surmounted by a gilt canopy, atop which is a Calvary scene, and figures of the Apostles. The central panels depict the Ascension, Resurrection, Assumption and Nativity, while the other panels depict scenes from the life of Jesus and parts of the Old Testament.

You exit the church under the curious wooden crocodile known as El Lagarto (the lizard), probably a replica of a gift from an Egyptian ruler wooing a Spanish *infanta*. The pretty **Patio de los Naranjos** is another Moorish original, formerly the ablutions courtyard of the mosque. It's shaded with the orange trees that give it its name, as well as an irrigation system likely to trip you as your eyes adjust from the dusky interior. Admire the lofty Puerta de la Concepción (20th century, but faithful to the cathedral's style) before you exit through the Puerta del Perdón.

## ★Real Alcázar

*Plaza del Triunfo s/n, T954-502323, www.alcazarsevilla.org. Oct-Mar 0930-1700, Apr-Sep 0930-1900. €9.50, students and retirees €2. The informative audio tour (Spanish, French, English, German, Italian) costs €3 and uses quotes from various kings responsible for the building's construction.*

Even if the delights of tapas and the heat of the day are seducing your hours in Sevilla away from you, don't head for home without seeing the Alcázar, as you'll be derided by any friends who have. While you'll see horseshoe arches, stucco, calligraphy and coffered ceilings throughout, it's not a Moorish palace. It used to be, but little remains from that period; it owes its Moorish look to the Castillian kings who built it after the Reconquest: Alfonso X and his enlightened son Pedro I.

As well as being a magnificent palace, the Alcázar was once a considerable fortress in this impressively fortified city, a fact easily appreciable as you pass through the chunky walls in the dramatic red Puerta del León entrance gate, named for the tiled king of beasts guarding it. You emerge on to a large courtyard dominated by the impressive façade of the main palace of the Castillian kings. Before heading into this, investigate the Patio del Yeso to the left, one of the few remaining Moorish structures, where lobed arches face horseshoe ones across a pool surrounded by myrtle hedges.

Opposite, across the courtyard, are chambers built by Fernando and Isabel to control New World affairs. Magellan planned his trip here, and there's an important *retablo* from this period of the Virgen de los Navegantes. In the main panel by Alejo Fernández, the Virgin spreads her protective mantle over Columbus, Carlos V, and a shadowy group of indigenous figures (who might see some trouble coming if they could glimpse the side panel of Santiago, Spain's patron, who is gleefully decapitating Moors).

From this main courtyard, if you arrive early, it is possible to see some of the **upper floor of the palace**, still used when Spanish royals are in town. A series of elaborately furnished chambers are visited on the **guided tour** ⓘ *€4.50, you can prebook (advisable) online or on T954-560040, which leaves roughly half-hourly.*

# Sevilla centre

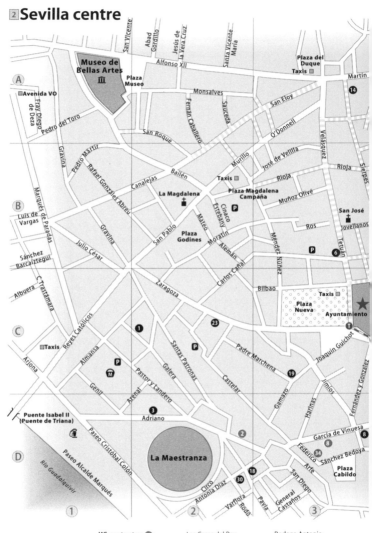

**Where to stay** 🛏
Adriano **1** *D2*
Alminar **2** *C4*
Corral del Rey **14** *C5*
EME Catedral **11** *D4*
Las Casas de los
  Mercaderes **6** *C4*

Las Casas del Rey
  de Baeza **9** *B6*
Simón **8** *D3*

**Restaurants** 🍴
Bar Alfalfa **2** *B5*
Bar Pepe Hillo **3** *D2*

Bodega Antonio
  Romero **30** *D2*
Casa La Viuda **6** *B3*
Casa Morales **8** *D3*
Casa Salva **15** *A1*
El Rinconcillo **20** *A6*
Enrique Becerra **19** *D3*

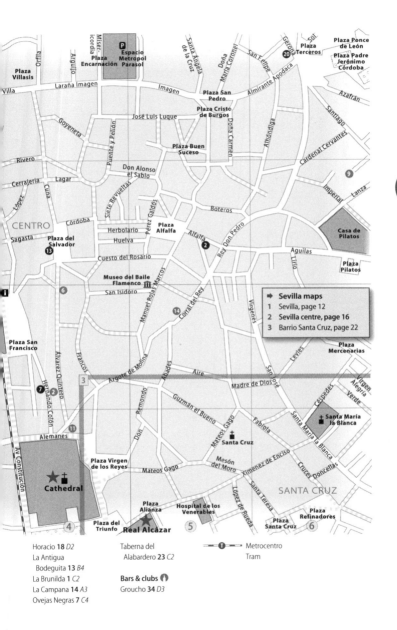

→ **Sevilla maps**

1 Sevilla, page 12
2 Sevilla centre, page 16
3 Barrio Santa Cruz, page 22

Horacio **18** *D2*
La Antigua
  Bodeguita **13** *B4*
La Brunilda **1** *C2*
La Campana **14** *A3*
Ovejas Negras **7** *C4*

Taberna del
  Alabardero **23** *C2*

**Bars & clubs** 🕐
Groucho **34** *D3*

━ **0** ━ Metrocentro
        Tram

## Semana Santa

Sevilla's Holy Week processions are an unforgettable sight. Mesmeric candlelit lines of hooded figures and cross-carrying penitents make their way through the streets accompanied by the mournful notes of a brass band and two large *pasos*, one with a scene from the Passion, one with a statue of Mary. These scenes aren't unusual in Spain but what makes it so special is the *sevillanos'* extraordinary respect and interest for the event and devotion to the sculptures.

In Sevilla at least, the Semana Santa processions we know today evolved when the Spanish crown lurched into financial meltdown in the 17th century, and Sevilla, the economic hub of the country, went with it. The idea that the city was being punished by God took hold. Public displays of penitence, and a projection of the people's suffering on to the weeping Mary or agonized Christ developed.

Today, members of nearly 60 *cofradías* (brotherhoods) practise intensively for their big moment, when they leave their home church or chapel and walk through the streets to the *carrera oficial*, a route leading along Calle Sierpes to the cathedral and then home again. Some of the brotherhoods have well over 1000 in the parade; these consist of *nazarenos*, who wear pointed hoods, *penitentes*, who carry crosses and *costaleros*, who carry the *pasos*. Each *paso* is accompanied by a band that plays haunting brass laments and deep thuds of drums.

The first brotherhoods walk on Palm Sunday and the processions continue up until Easter Sunday, when a single *cofradía* celebrates the Resurrection. The most important processions are on the night of Maundy Thursday (*la madrugá*), when several brotherhoods go to the cathedral during the wee hours.

*Sevillanos* hold the processions in great esteem and a high percentage are members of a *cofradía*, even if they're not really religious. Everyone has their favourite sculpture too; the best-loved Marys are La Macarena and La Triana. The most admired Christs are El Cachorro and Jesús del Gran Poder, both supreme pieces of art. During the processions, it's not uncommon for people on the street or on balconies to launch into a *saeta*, a haunting flamenco-based song inspired by the *paso*; similarly, the Marys are often greeted with shouts of '*Guapa!*'.

### What to take

Pick up a copy of the programme for the processions; it's available free in bookshops. Buy a map with a street index so you can track down exactly what route the processions take. Make sure you're dosed up with suncream if it's a hot day, but don't bother with an umbrella; the *cofradías* stay home if it's wet, as the rain damages the *pasos*. They have to wait until the next year.

### What to see

If you're in Sevilla for the week, you'll see plenty of processions. Just pick a couple to start the week, and then go at it hard on the Thursday night. The busiest places are near the church and cathedral (although the *carrera oficial*, the last stretch into the cathedral, is seating only). There are less people on the *cofradía*'s return journey.

The seating along the *carrera oficial* is mostly occupied by long-time local subscribers, but there are some seats available, which you can nab by going in the early morning and paying the attendants. The price is usually €25-50. The view is great, but it can be boring sitting in one place; much of the excitement is in seeking out the *cofradías* or coming across them by chance in a narrow street. Some of the most interesting are:

**La Paz** (Palm Sunday)  The first *cofradía* and a spectacular sight coming up Calle San Fernando, best seen from the fountain in Puerta de Jerez, where it passes around 1500.

**San Esteban** (Tuesday)  Their exit (1500) and entry (2230-2330) from a church just behind the Casa de Pilatos is great to watch as the manouevring of the *pasos* is a difficult feat. Get there a long time before.

**Las Siete Palabras** (Wednesday)  This 16th-century *cofradía* has an excellent Calvary as one of their *pasos*. Be in the Museo de Bellas Artes square from 2030.

**La Madrugá**  Late on Thursday night, six of the most important *cofradías* make the journey. It's worth making the effort to stay up all night, as most of the city does. First up is El Silencio, a 14th-century brotherhood and one of the oldest. Although it's not completely silent, it's black-robed *nazarenos* are an eerie sight. See it from Plaza del Duque from 0100 and stay there for Jesús del Gran Poder, whose stunning Christ follows hard on their heels. Then trot north to the Alameda de Hércules, for the procession of La Macarena. At about 0430 try and be at the Puente de Triana to watch her great rival La Esperanza de Triana cross the river. If you're still on two feet, head to Plaza Encarnación to see Los Gitanos, the well-loved gypsy *cofradía*.

**El Cachorro/La O** (Friday)  These two popular Triana *cofradías* simultaneously cross the Puente de San Telmo and the Puente de Triana on their way home at 2330 or so.

**La Resurrección** (Sunday)  Leaving their Macarena home at 0400-0500, they reach the cathedral about 0800, where there's enough room to see them, the last of the processions.

### Etiquette
Be silent when watching the *pasos* pass, and don't applaud unless other people are so doing. It is considered rude to cross a procession; definitely don't do it in front of the *paso* or among the band.

### Timing
If you've got to be somewhere at a certain time during Semana Santa, allow plenty of it, as you're likely to get caught in crowds watching a procession. It can take ages to get even a short distance.

### What to eat
Semana Santa food is *torrijas*, bread slices soaked in milk and honey and fried, *pestiños*, fried nuggets of honey and dough, and the offcuts of communion hosts.

## BACKGROUND

## Sevilla

While Sevilla legend attributes the founding of the city to Hercules, it is likely that the first permanent settlements on this site were built by the Tartessians in the first half of the first millennium BC.

The Phoenicians established themselves here shortly afterwards, and they extended and fortified the existing town. It became an important trading centre in the Western Mediterranean, and continued to be so after a Carthaginian takeover in the third century BC. In 206 BC the Romans defeated them in the battle of Ilipa, near the city that they named Hispalis. They also established the town of Itálica nearby, originally as a rest camp for mutinous Italian soldiers. The river in these days was known as the Betis. Caesar arrived here as administrator of the town and enjoyed his stay by all accounts. The people sided with him against Pompeii and were rewarded by being conferred full Roman citizenship. When Augustus created the province of Baetica, Hispalis soon became the capital, and both it and Itálica became very important Roman cities. The emperor Trajan was born in the latter and Hadrian grew up there. Christianity took early root in Sevilla and, after early persecutions, soon flourished.

The city was sacked by Vandals and Swabians as the Empire collapsed, but then prospered under Visigothic rule, with the wise historian and archbishop San Isidoro particularly prominent. The Islamic invasion in 711 put an end to the Visigothic kingdom; Hispalis was transliterated to Isbiliyya, from which Sevilla is derived, and the river was renamed *al wadi al kibir* (big river), or Guadalquivir as it is now written. Sevilla spent the first few centuries of the Moorish occupation under the shadow of Córdoba, but, on the collapse of the caliphate, became an independent *taifa* state and grew rapidly to be the most powerful one in Al-Andalus. Under the poet-king Al-Mu'tamid, the city experienced an exceptional flourishing of wealth and culture. Much of Sevilla's Moorish architectural heritage dates from the 12th century and the Almohad regime.

The palace façade is a fusion of Christian and Moorish styles that just about achieves harmony. Inscriptions about the glory of Allah (Pedro had a deep interest in Islamic culture) adjoin more conventional Latin ones proclaiming royal greatness.

This fusion is repeated throughout this whole section, centred around the stunning **Patio de las Doncellas**. Throughout the complex are azulejos, topped by friezes of ceramic decoration, while higher up, intricate stucco friezes are surmounted by a range of marvellous inlaid ceilings. Also worth admiring are the imposing doors, some elaborately inlaid. Among the rooms off this courtyard are the **Salón de Embajadores**, with a beautiful half-orange ceiling and a frieze of Spanish kings; and the chapel, where Carlos V married his first cousin Isabella of Portugal (one of many inbreedings that doomed the Habsburg line).

In 1248, Isbiliyya was conquered by Fernando III, and nearly all its Muslim population were expelled and their lands divided among noble families. In 1391, a massive anti-Jewish pogrom occurred in the city. Synagogues were forcibly changed into churches and the Jewish quarter virtually ceased to exist. The current cathedral was begun soon afterwards.

With the discovery of the New World, Sevilla's Golden Age began. In 1503, it was granted a monopoly on trade with the transatlantic colonies, and became one of the largest and most prosperous cities in Europe.

The 17th century, however, saw a decline, although this was the zenith of Sevilla's school of painting, with artists such as Zurbarán, Murillo and Velázquez all operating. The expulsion of the *moriscos* (converted Moors) in 1610 hit the city hard and merchants left to ply their trade elsewhere. A plague in 1649 killed an incredible half of the inhabitants, and in 1717, with the Guadalquivir silting up rapidly, New World trade was moved to Cádiz.

Occupied by the French from 1810-1812, Sevilla only really rose from its torpor in the 20th century. The massive Ibero-American exhibition of 1929 bankrupted the city but created the infrastructure for a modern town and many fine public spaces. In the Civil War, the oddball General Queipo de Llano bluffed his way into control of the city. Workers struggled against the rising and were brutally repressed, with much of Triana destroyed.

In 1982, the Sevillano Felipe González was elected the first Socialist prime minister since the Civil War, governing until 1996. The city, beginning to stir once more, hosted a World Cup semi-final and, 10 years later, Expo 1992, having already become the capital of semi-autonomous Andalucía. The event left the city with enormous debts but attracted some 15 million visitors and boosted Sevilla's international profile.

The city continues with urban improvements, with the metro and tram system recently inaugurated, and extensive pedestrianization of the old centre implemented. Unemployment, poverty and homelessness are still massive, if not always visible, problems.

Adjacent is the **Renaissance Palace**, heavily altered from the original Gothic by Carlos V and his descendants. In the chapel is an interesting Velázquez portraying a beautiful Virgin placing a chasuble over the shoulders of San Ildefonso. From here stretches the vast and fantastic garden; different sections filled with slurping carp, palm trees and a grotesque gallery built into a section of the old walls. Steps lead down to the picturesque covered pool known as **Los Baños de Doña María de Padilla**. The garden has featured in several films and series, most recently in *Game of Thrones*. You finally exit the complex through the vestibule where coaches and horses used to roll in, and you emerge in the Patio de Bandera. There are often small exhibitions in this last section.

## Archivo de las Indias
*Plaza del Triunfo s/n, T954-500528. Mon-Sat 0930-1645, Sun 1000-1400. Free.*

This square and sober Renaissance building – "An immense icebox of granite guarded by lions, in which is housed the colonial past, every sigh and every comma, until the end of the world" (C Nooteboom, *Roads to Santiago*) – between the cathedral and Alcázar was once Sevilla's Lonja, where merchants met to broker trade with the New World. The cannons poking out from the roof echo the decks of Spain's ocean-going vessels.

In the late 18th century it was converted into the state archive, where all documents relating to the Americas were stored and filed, an intriguing record that includes everything from the excited scribblings of Columbus to the most mundane book-keeping of remote jungle outposts. There's a small display of

**3** **Barrio Santa Cruz**

**Where to stay** 🛏
Amadeus & La Música **1** *B4*
Apartamentos Murillo **3** *C3*
Casa del Poeta **2** *B3*
El Rey Moro **12** *C3*
Goya **8** *B3*
Las Casas de
 la Judería **15** *B5*
Pensión
 San Pancracio **18** *B4*

**Restaurants** 🍴
Bodega Santa Cruz **4** *C2*
Carmela **5** *B4*
La Goleta **8** *B2*
Las Teresas **10** *C3*

the building's history on the ground floor, and upstairs, under the vaulted stone ceilings and among the polished shelves holding the archives are regular themed exhibitions and a couple of Goya portraits. Researchers can examine documents in the reading room, after filling in a form and showing ID.

## Barrio Santa Cruz

Sevilla's most charming barrio: small plazas shaded by orange trees

Once home to much of Sevilla's Jewish population, atmospheric Barrio Santa Cruz has a web of narrow pedestrian lanes. Squeezed between the Alcázar, cathedral and a section of the old city walls, it's very touristy but thankfully not over-prettified, and there's a fairly standard tour beat that you can easily explore away from. There are excellent accommodation and restaurant options as well as several intriguing antique and handicraft shops; even the souvenir shops are comparatively tasteful.

The best way to enter the barrio is from the Plaza del Triunfo by the cathedral; head through the gate in the Alcázar walls to the south into the pretty square of Patio de Banderas, floored with sand and lined with orange trees. In the opposite corner, duck through a small tunnel and twist and turn your way on to Calle Judería, one of the nooks with most medieval flavour.

A wander through the narrow lanes of Barrio Santa Cruz will reveal much. On one side, the area is bounded by a stretch of the old Almohad city walls, behind which is the public park of the Jardines de Murillo, centred around a monument to Columbus. Nearby, Calle Santa María la Blanca was once one of the city's entrances; the food markets used to be in this zone and farmers would enter here with carts piled high with meats, cereals, and vegetables. These days, it's more of a plaza than a street, with several sun-kissed terraces (go for Carmela ahead of any place with paellas on display). It's well worth

---

**Sevilla maps**
1 Sevilla, page 12
2 Sevilla centre, page 16
3 Barrio Santa Cruz, page 22

González de León

Verde

⑮

Santa María la Blanca
✝

Archeros

Plaza Curtidores

Doncellas

Caño y Cueto

Menéndez Pelayo

**Puerta de la Carne**

**Murillo**

Paseo Catalina de Ribera

To Prado San Sebastián
Bus Station

⑤                    ⑥

Taberna Poncio **2** *B4*

**Bars & clubs**
The Second Room **1** *A1*

visiting the small **church** ⓘ *Mon-Fri 1000-1300, 1600-2000*, that gives the street its name. The attractive toothed arch of the portal gives little hint of the Baroque fantasy inside – the central vault of the triple-naved church is carved with a riot of floral and vegetal decoration. In the left aisle you'll see a Murillo, a *Last Supper* that's not usually reckoned one of his best works but certainly deserves to be. A young, visionary Christ is surrounded by the wise, bearded old heads of his apostles. It's all the better for being in situ.

## Hospital de los Venerables
*Plaza de los Venerables 8, T954-562696, www.focus.abengoa.es. Daily 1000-1400, 1600-2000. €5.50, free Sun afternoon.*

In the heart of Barrio Santa Cruz, and built at the end of the 17th century in a charitable vein, the Venerables refers to the old priests for whom it was originally intended as a hospital and residence. Now owned and managed by a cultural foundation, the building regularly holds good temporary exhibitions on Sevillian culture and history, but is also worth visiting for its church, a repository of fine painting of the late Sevillian school. The church is alongside the main courtyard, a noble space centred around a sunken fountain and surrounded by an arcade on marble columns. Stunning tilework completes the effect. Entry includes an audio tour.

## Aire de Sevilla
*C Aire 15, T955-010024, www.airedesevilla.com. Daily 1000-midnight, to 0200 weekends, tea room 1530-2400, 0200 at weekends. Visit with aromatherapy €26, with massage €41.*

Located in a 16th-century palace, this luxurious Arabian-style bathhouse offers warm, hot, and cold baths as well as a steam room and massage facilities. The place itself is beautifully relaxing, with delicate lighting and stylish design. Only a certain number of people are allowed in at a time, so it pays to reserve a slot in advance by phone or via the website. Take a bathing suit; you can hire one if necessary.

## Centro de Interpretación Judería de Sevilla
*C Ximénez de Enciso 22, T954-047089, www.juderiadesevilla.es. Mon-Sat 1030-1530, 1700-2000, Sun 1030-1930. €6.50.*

This is run by enthusiastic people and has a reasonable display on Sevilla's Jewish history, with information about various historical figures. It's set in a beautiful Santa Cruz house. They also run walking tours (€22 including museum entry) of the former Jewish barrio.

Much of this area is taken up with the large Parque María Luisa, donated to the city by the queen's sister in the late 19th century. It was used as the site for the grandiose 1929 Ibero-American Exhibition, an event on a massive scale that the dictatorship hoped would re-establish Sevilla and Spain in the world spotlight. The legacy of the exhibition is a much-loved public park, the monumental Plaza de España, and a beautiful series of the former pavilions. On Calle San Fernando, the massive and elegant Hotel Alfonso XIII was built to put up important visitors to the exhibition.

### Antigua Fábrica de Tabacos
*C San Fernando 4, T954-551000. Mon-Fri 0800-2030. Free.*

Next door to the Alfonso XIII hotel stands what was once Spain's second largest building, surrounded by a fence and moat; the building was originally the cigarette factory and workers were carefully checked to make sure they didn't nick any fags. Visitors flocked to the cigarette factory in the late 19th century to see the girls at work, for it had been made famous by *Carmen* and other tales of the beauty of Sevilla's womenfolk. Despite poor conditions, the workers must have had no complaints about the building itself, with numerous elegant hallways and courtyards that suit it perfectly in its new function as a university building. It's a lively place and worth a visit to wander around its corridors.

### ★Parque María Luisa
*Daily 0800-2400 summer (2200 winter). Free.*

This beautiful and peaceful space is Sevilla's best park, again developed for the 1929 exhibition. It's full of quiet corners, even on busy days, and a series of informative plaques detail the huge range of exotic trees and plants on show; parts of the park even feel like an authentic rainforest.

Around the park are dotted various buildings erected for the 1929 exhibition. The most grandiose of these is the Plaza de España, envisaged as a second Giralda, a symbol of a new, dynamic Sevilla. The semi-circular area is backed by a massive brick and marble building that curves around to two proud towers. A small canal was once used for leisurely rowing and is crossed by four bridges. The most endearing feature is the row of benches, each one dedicated to one of Spain's provinces. A tiled map of each is accompanied by a significant historical event and some typical symbols. The buildings are used now for various government departments, but it's no surprise that the stunning ensemble has been used in several films, featuring as part of Cairo in *Lawrence of Arabia* and, more recently, Naboo in *Star Wars: The Attack of the Clones* and Wadiya in *The Dictator*.

At the other end of the park are two excellent museums. The **Museo de Artes y Costumbres Populares** ⓘ *Plaza de América 3, T954-232576, mid-Sep to mid-Jun*

## ON THE ROAD
## Feria de Abril

Sevilla's April fiesta is a lively counterpoint to the solemnity of the Semana Santa processions. Originally a gypsy horse fair, it took its present form in the early 20th century. It gets bigger and livelier every year; with the well-loved Los Remedios grounds being squeezed to the limit by well over 1000 *casetas*, the event is eventually scheduled to move to a new location in a few years' time.

The *casetas* are colourfully striped tents, venues for six days of socializing, eating, drinking *manzanilla* and dancing *sevillanas*. Most are privately owned, by social clubs, employers or families; bar a few public ones, entry is by invitation only. It's busy day and night; during the afternoon *sevillanos* dashingly dressed in riding suits and bright *flamenca* costumes parade by in colourful carriages, while the dancing and drinking action hots up at night. A large funfair adds to the attraction as do the season's biggest bullfights, held at the Maestranza.

**Getting there** The massive Feria gate is at the bottom of Calle Asunción, a 15-minute walk from the Puente de San Telmo. Shuttle buses run from Prado San Sebastián station. Cars are not allowed near the grounds. Taxis are, but you're much better walking home as the queues are horrendous. Or use the rank at the back exit rather than by the front gate.

**Kick-off** The Feria begins on the Monday night two weeks and a day after Easter Sunday (unless this would mean that it begins in May, in which case it's brought forward). Crowds wait until midnight, when the gate (a new one is built each year) is spectacularly lit up and the party begins. The Feria runs until the next Sunday, when a fireworks display east of the gate officially ends the revelry at midnight.

**Casetas** Grab a map from tourist information; most of the public *casetas* are clearly marked; these belong to leftist political parties and the local

Tue-Sat 1000-2030, Sun 1000-1700, mid-Jun to mid-Sep Tue-Sun 1000-1700, free for EU citizens, €1.50 others, is in the rather majestic *mudéjar* pavilion. The exhibition is a cut above the dreary displays that well-intentioned ethnographic museums often seem to become. The top floor is mostly devoted to what *sevillanos* wore through the centuries; there's a good blend of period paintings and costumes themselves. There's an excellent display on wheat farming, important here since the Stone Age, and a collection of Semana Santa and Feria posters.

In the massive basement are many items of furniture and household use, as well as reconstructions of typical workshops, including a guitar maker's, and a wine bodega whose smell permeates the level. The information is in Spanish but it's all pretty self-explanatory and a fascinating record of urban and rural Sevilla life.

Sevilla's **Museo Arqueológico** ① *Pabellón de Bellas Artes, Plaza de América s/n, T954-232401, mid-Sep to May Tue-Sat 1000-2030, Sun 1000-1700, mid-Jun to Sep Tue-Sun 1000-1700, free for EU citizens, €1.50 otherwise*, should be good, considering the wealth of peoples that have lived and traded in the region since prehistoric times. And it doesn't disappoint, with a particularly rich Roman collection.

councils of the city. If you know a local that can invite you in to a *caseta*, well and good, but it's fairly easy to get in to some of the less exclusive ones; after all, many of them are happy to have a few extra punters paying for drinks and thus defraying their hire costs.

Dress respectably and ask the doorman politely in Spanish if you can enter; you'll get plenty of knockbacks but also plenty of entries, particularly (doormen being doormen) if a woman does the asking. Large groups of people speaking English will likely get in nowhere. Up until about 2100, there are no doormen, and many of the *casetas* can be entered freely.

**Eating and drinking** The best places to eat are the *casetas* themselves, which put on a range of good-value tapas and *raciones*. Drink *manzanilla* (usually served in a half-bottle) or *rebujito*, a weaker refreshing blend of the same with lemonade, served in a litre cup. *Pescaíto frito* (fried fish) is traditionally eaten on the first night of Feria.

In all the *casetas*, once the eating's done, people spend most of the night dancing. The *sevillana* is a relatively modern form with roots in both flamenco and Latin music. A dance has four distinct parts, all characterized by elaborate arms-aloft movements, partners stepping around each other, and stares of moody intensity. You'll experience another dimension of Feria if you manage to learn the basics.

**Kicking on** Unless you've hit a manic *caseta*, Feria winds down about 0300. If you want more, the best places are around the Feria grounds on and near Calle Asunción; the rest of Sevilla's nightlife is comparatively quiet during Feria. The biggest night at Feria is usually the Friday; Saturday isn't nearly as busy.

**Toilets** Queues in the public *casetas* are long, so you're better going in a private one, paying €1 to use one of the few public loos around, or dashing off to the trees at the edge of the compound.

Among a good selection of prehistoric finds and fossils the standout pieces are from Tartessian culture; a people that lived in the Guadalquivir valley from about 1100 BC onwards. Their best pieces, finely worked pottery, carved stone and gold jewellery, show clear influences from the Phoenicians, who began trading along this coast around 700 BC.

On the ground floor, after an imposing array of Iberian stone lions, come the Roman finds, mostly from nearby Itálica, but many also from the large necropolis at Carmona. There are several mosaics; one from Ecija depicting Bacchus and his leashed pards, and a later one showing the Judgement of Paris, with Aphrodite seeming keen to win the contest. Among the excellent sculptures on display are a second-century AD headless Venus, striding out of the waves at the moment of her birth, a slightly later Diana, the emperor Trajan in full heroic mode, and a fine depiction of the bearded Hadrian. There's a collection of citizens' portrait heads – a real rogues' gallery – and a fascinating room full of bronze law scrolls. There are English summaries at the entrance to most rooms, and a good printed handout.

## Triana

★Many visitors find that Triana becomes their favourite part of Sevilla. It's redolent with history from every epoch of the Christian city as well as having a picturesque riverfront lined with terraced bars and restaurants. It was for a long time the gypsy barrio and as such the home of flamenco in Sevilla. Although most of the gypsies were moved on in the 1950s, its backstreet bars are still the best place to catch impromptu performances. Triana is also famous for ceramics; most of the azulejo tiles that decorate Sevilla's houses so beautifully come from here, and there are still many workshops in the area. It's also got a significant maritime history.

Entering the barrio across the Puente Isabel II, you arrive at Plaza de Altozano. From here, Calle Betis stretches to your left along the riverfront and is one of the top strolls in the city, lined with prettily coloured buildings, most of which are dedicated to eating and drinking.

Behind here, on Calle Pureza, is the **Iglesia de Santa Ana** ① *C Pureza s/n, Mon-Fri 1030-1330, plus Tue-Wed 1630-1830, €1.50 donation requested*. The 'Cathedral of Triana' is believed to be Sevilla's oldest church, dating from around 1276.

Not far from here, at Calle Pureza 53, La Esperanza de Triana lives in an ornate *retablo* behind the big yellow and white façade of the **Capilla de los Marineros** ① *Mon-Sat 1000-1330, 1730-2100, Sun 1000-1400, 1730-2030, free.* She and La Macarena are the two most-adored Virgins of the city, and there are few bars around without a picture up of one or the other of them. Her passages across the bridges in the wee hours of Good Friday morning are among the most emotional of the Semana Santa processions; see box, page 18.

On the other side of Triana, the **Capilla de Patrocinio** ① *C Castilla 182, Mon-Fri 1030-1330, 1800-2130, Sun 1030-1330, free*, is worth a visit for the superb Christ inside, who is much revered across Sevilla. He is named El Cachorro, after a dead young gypsy that the sculptor is said to have used as a model. The sculpture is breathtaking; you can feel the sinews of the crucified Christ straining, while his face is a perfectly rendered mixture of anguish and relief.

## El Arenal

If you look at a picture of Sevilla in the early 19th century or before, you'll see that from the Moorish Torre del Oro, the city wall recedes from the riverbank, leaving a large open area, El Arenal (meaning sandy spot). This was a haunt of thieves, swindlers, prostitutes and smugglers, who hung out near the docks where the action was. It was built over in the 19th century, and El Arenal is now one of Sevilla's most pleasant barrios, with some of the city's major landmarks.

## Torre del Oro
*Paseo de Colón, T954-222419. Mon-Fri 0930-1845, Sat-Sun 1030-1845. €3, free Mon.*

The spiky battlements of this beautiful Moorish tower are one of Sevilla's primary landmarks and the building is powerfully evocative of the city's military and maritime history. The exterior was once decorated with bright golden ceramic tiles, from which it gets its name. The interior now holds a motley maritime museum with sharks' teeth and paintings of galleons and sea-dogs that aren't illuminated by any explanatory panels. It's worth going in, however, for the great river views from the top and for the old prints showing Sevilla in the late 16th century: Triana has its boat-bridge and castle, and the docks are bristling with ships.

## La Maestranza
*Paseo de Colón 12, T954-224577, www.realmaestranza.com. Daily Nov-Apr 0930-1900, May and Oct 0930-2000, Jun-Aug 0930-2300, except bullfight days (Sun in spring and summer and all week during Feria), when it's open 0930-1500, guided tours every 30 mins (English and Spanish). €7.*

One of Spain's principal temples of bullfighting, La Maestranza is a beautiful building wedged into a city block, which accounts for its slightly elliptical shape. Started in the mid-18th century, it took until the late 1800s to finish it. It holds some 14,000 spectators, and sells out nearly every seat during the April Feria, when the most prestigious fights of the season are held. The Sevilla crowd are among the most knowledgeable of aficionados, and many of bullfighting's most famous names have been *sevillanos*. The guided tour is a poor substitute for the atmosphere at the corridas, and has no information on how a bullfight works. The main entrance, La Puerta del Príncipe, has an imposing wrought-iron gateway by Pedro Roldán; it's a 16th-century work that originally stood in a convent. If a *torero* has a particularly good day, he is carried out through this door. There's a small museum, which has some good pictures of the chaotic affairs that were early bullfights before the present structure of a fight was adopted in 1830. You also briefly visit the horse stables, but disappointingly not the bullpens. Nor are you permitted on to the sand itself. You do, however, see the small chapel, where bullfighters can pray before the fight, and the infirmary, a chillingly modern room where horn wounds are operated on.

## Hospital de Caridad
*C Temprado 3, T954-223223. Mon-Sat 0900-1300, 1530-1900, Sun 0900-1230. €5.*

Behind the theatre is this *residencia de ancianos* (nursing home) still fulfilling its original charitable purpose. It was built as a hospital for the poor by Miguel de Mañara, a curious 17th-century *sevillano* often likened to Don Juan. After a scandalous youth of seduction and deceit he reformed completely when he saw a vision of his own death and dedicated himself to a life of charity and religion. He had a good eye for art; as a result of this, the hospital chapel has a collection of masterpieces commissioned by Mañara expressly to remind his brotherhood of the charitable virtues and the ultimate futility of worldly wealth and pride.

Two astonishing paintings stand above and opposite the entrance. They are the two finest, and most disturbing, works of the Sevillian painter Juan de Valdés Leal. The first one you'll see depicts a leering skeletal Death with a scythe, putting out a candle with one hand while trampling over objects that represent worldly wealth, power, and knowledge. The inscription *In Ictu Oculi* translates as in the blink of an eye. Opposite this is an even more challenging painting entitled *Finis Gloriae Mundi* (the end of worldly glory). It depicts a crypt in which a dead bishop and knight are being eaten by worms. Above, a balance is borne by the hand of Christ. On one side are symbols of the seven deadly sins, on the other side symbols of a holy love between God and Christ. 'Neither more nor less', read the words on the scales. Mañara commissioned these works in detail, and the face of the knight is thought to be his own.

After these grim warnings, the paintings of Murillo demonstrate the charitable life Mañara wanted his brotherhood to lead. Although four are missing (they were stolen by Napoleon's pillaging general, Soult, and are now scattered around the world; they include the impressive *Return of the Prodigal Son* in Washington), those that remain are exceptional examples of this artist's work. St John of God carries a sick man, while St Isabelle of Hungary cares for the afflicted. A Moses horned with light brings forth water from the rock, while Jesus feeds the multitude with loaves and fishes. In a *retablo* by Bernardo Simón de Pineda next to the pulpit is another Murillo painting, a depiction of the Annunciation. The sculptor Pedro Roldán is responsible for the figures in the intense *retablo* of Santo Cristo de la Caridad, with a Christ dripping blood flanked by cherubs. The main *retablo*, a Churrigueresque riot of cherubs and *salomónica* columns, is again the work of Roldán and Pineda; the former responsible for the emotive central tableau of the burial of Christ.

Juan de Valdés Leal painted the ceiling, of which the cupola is particularly fine, while Murillo also painted the small panels of the infants Jesus and John the Baptist above two other *retablos*.

## Centro and San Vicente

Sevilla's shopping heartland

The busy Centro region is centred on the shopping streets of Sierpes, Tetuán, Velásquez, Cuna and O'Donnell. It's a fascinating stroll around this area, and there's an encouragingly low number of chain stores, giving the zone a particularly local character. Shops selling fans, shawls and other Sevilla fashion essentials abound. Worth looking for is the small church of San José, on Calle Jovellanos just off Calle Sierpes; the main *retablo*, an extraordinary sight: with its two side panels and bristling with cherubs, it could be a production of *A Midsummer Night's Dream* in gold.

## ★El Ayuntamiento

*Plaza Nueva s/n, T954-590101. Mon-Thu 1630-1930, Sat 1000 (subject to change due to civic functions and other events). €4, free Sat. Bring passport or ID to enter. Closed Jul-Aug.*

It's hard to miss Sevilla's town hall as it fronts two major squares, Plaza Nueva and Plaza San Francisco. It was formerly the site of one of Sevilla's most important monasteries; in the disentailment of 1835, it was demolished and the hitherto tiny Ayuntamiento expanded. As such, the building has two distinct sections, a Plateresque and a neoclassical (as well as some more recent annexes). From Plaza San Francisco, you can admire the superbly intricate stonework of the original 16th-century building. The architect of the newer structure thought he'd better continue with the Plateresque design to ensure harmony, but was stopped in his tracks by outraged neoclassicists appalled at the perceived flippancy; the Plateresque stonework thus comes to an abrupt and jagged end.

The interior, entered through the sober façade on Plaza Nueva, is a revelation. An excellent volunteer-guided tour (Spanish only, but worth doing even if you don't understand the commentary) visits the chambers of the original edifice, which has some breathtaking Renaissance stonework that still features some Gothic influences. The lower council chamber is entered through a dignified doorway crowned with a depiction of Fernando III; inside there's an amazing coffered stone ceiling with busts of 36 monarchs in the coffers, finishing with Carlos V himself in one corner, complete with imperial crown. There are several elegant rooms on the top floor; notable works of art up here include a Zurbarán *Inmaculada* and a sketch by Murillo.

## Espacio Metropol Parasol

*Plaza de la Encarnación, www.espacio-metropol.com. Viewing platform Sun-Thu 1030-0000, Fri-Sat 1030-0100, €3 including a drink. Museum Tue-Sat 1000-2000, Sun 1000-1400, €2.10.*

This striking and controversial addition to central Sevilla opened in 2011 and has a viewing platform that is a magical place to be at sunset. Consisting of six giant interlinked parasol-like structures – dubbed Las Setas (the mushrooms) by locals – it was designed by Jürgen Mayer. The lower gallery holds the traditional food market and an archaeological museum based around the Roman remains discovered below street level. From here you can access the viewing platform in a lift. It's a spectacular series of walkways that puts you up among the city's rooftops, giving great views in all directions.

## ★Casa de Pilatos

*Plaza de Pilatos s/n, T954-225298. Daily 0900-1900, to 1800 winter. €6 lower floor, €8 both floors, free Wed from 1500 for EU citizens.*

This stunning mansion is still partly inhabited by members of the family of the Dukes of Medinaceli, who built most of it in the late 15th to early 16th centuries. It owes its name to the story that the Duke, on a pilgrimage to Jerusalem, was so struck by the former residence of the Roman governors (including Pontius Pilate) that he decided to model his own house on it. The profusion of classical sculpture decorating the courtyards and gardens, some of it original, certainly gives the house a Roman air, but the architecture is principally an attractive blend of Renaissance classicism and *mudéjar* styles. Sensitive restoration has healed the damage caused during the Spanish Civil War, when the building was used as a hospital.

The highlight of the visit is the central courtyard, reached from the entrance by passing under a thriving purple cascade of bougainvillea. It's a stunning combination of azulejos and stuccowork; the Italianate central fountain is overseen by statues, including an excellent Athena Promachos. On the walls are mounted a series of Roman portrait heads, obtained by the dukes from Italy. The gardens are beautiful and peaceful; one even has a small grotto with tinkling water. The staircase to the upper level is a cascade of shining tiles topped by a majestic golden dome that owes some of its decoration to Moorish *mocárabes*.

Beyond here is accessed by a **guided tour** ⓘ *English and Spanish, tours leave every 30 mins from 1000-1830 except 1400 and 1430*. The tour takes you through furnished rooms with some excellent 17th-century coffered ceilings and a large collection of paintings, including a Goya of the Ronda bullring, and an Assumption by Murillo, not one of his better works.

### Museo del Baile Flamenco
*C Manuel Rojas Marcos 3, T954-340311, www.museoflamenco.com. Daily 1000-1900. €10.*

This museum is devoted to flamenco, in particular the dance side of it, and involved renowned *bailaora* Cristina Hoyos in its development. Set in a lovely patioed building, it's a good spot to visit before you see some performances. While the entrance charge offers questionable value, there are stylish interactive displays on the world of flamenco dance, with an interestingly humanistic slant: dancers' lives are examined as well as the great performances. They have decent evening shows daily. There's also a shop and café.

### ★Museo de Bellas Artes
*Plaza del Museo 9, T954-221829. Mid-Sep to May Tue-Sat 1000-2030, Sun 1000-1700, mid-Jun to mid-Sep Tue-Sun 1000-1700. Free for EU citizens, €1.50 for others.*

Sevilla's major art gallery is a must-see, picturesquely housed in a convent dating from the 17th and 18th centuries. This is appropriate enough, as most of the collection comes from the monasteries stripped of all their possessions in the Disentailment Act of 1835. The Sevillian school of painting was the dominant artistic force in Spain's Golden Age and is represented here in all its glory, offset by peaceful and pretty tiled patios.

The collection is thoughtfully laid out and thankfully uncluttered. Early pieces include a fine work from the monastery of San Agustín by Martín de Vos showing the awakening dead being sorted by angels and demons. In the same room there's also an El Greco; a good portrait of his own son.

In the early years of the 17th century, two distinct styles were evident in Sevillian painting, naturalism and mannerism, but these were gradually brought together as the century progressed. The latter style is well represented here by a selection of Francisco Pacheco's works. A portrait by the master Velázquez (Pacheco's son-in-law), of a gentleman against a brooding sky, is also in this section. Room IV has works of another mannerist, Alonso Vázquez, including, appropriately, a series on San Pedro Nolasco, who founded the original monastery on this site.

The former convent church is an awesome space with an elaborate painted ceiling. Here we see the evolution of the Sevilla school to its peak; the works of Zurbarán and Murillo. Although the former is represented here by an appropriately imposing heavenly Father and his large, famous Apotheosis of St Thomas Aquinas, there are more of his works upstairs; this room belongs to Murillo, whose statue graces the square outside the museum. Most of his works here are from the former Capuchin monastery. The city's patrons, Santa Justa and Santa Rufina, hold the Giralda in one renowned canvas, while a tender San Felix and child, *St Francis' Dream of the Crucified Christ*, and the famous *Virgin of the Napkin*, who holds a wide-eyed Christ child, are other noteworthy pieces. While mannerist traces remain in his early work, Murillo evolves into a complete Baroque style characterized by intense religious fervour, usually centred on a gaze or glance of striking power or emotion.

There are more Murillos upstairs and a long gallery devoted to Juan de Valdés Leal (1622-1690). Zurbarán, a little out of context, is represented in Room X. In the corridor outside is perhaps his most powerful work here, a crucifixion of incredible solitude and force, with Christ, head-down, seemingly chiselled from rock.

The 19th- and 20th-century rooms have works by Sevillian proto-Impressionist Gonzalo Bilbao as well as a portrait of the haunted Romantic poet Gustavo Adolfo Bécquer, famously and sensitively portrayed by his brother Valeriano, while two good portraits by the Basque painter Ignacio Zuloaga and a fiesta scene by Gustavo Bacarisas round off the superb collection.

## La Macarena
working-class barrio with Sevilla's best markets and buzzing nightlife

★The large barrio of La Macarena, once one of the poorest slums in the peninsula, is an enticing web of narrow streets and numerous churches and chapels, occupying the northern portion of the old town. One church is home to Sevilla's best-loved Virgin, La Esperanza de la Macarena. She gives her name to many of Sevilla's women, one of whom was the subject of the bestselling Latin hit of all time, by the ageing duo Los del Río. Still a working-class zone, La Macarena is home to much of Sevilla's alternative culture. It's still demarcated by a long section of the city wall, the best-preserved chunk of what was once one of Europe's mightiest bastions.

## Walking tour of Barrio La Macarena

Heading into the barrio along Calle Santa Vicente María, you come to the **Iglesia de San Lorenzo y Jesús del Gran Poder** ⓘ *mid-Sep to mid-Jun Mon-Thu 0900-1330, 1800-2100, Fri 0730-2200, Sat-Sun 0800-1330, 1800-2100, mid-Jun to mid-Sep Mon-Thu 0800-1330, 1800-2100, Fri 0730-1400, 1700-2200, Sat-Sun 0800-1400, 1800-2100, free*, most notable for the 17th-century sculpture of Christ by Juan de Mesa in a side chapel. It's a focus of much local adoration and a breathtaking piece of art; Jesus looks utterly careworn and harrowed; the brotherhood's procession with the sculpture is one of the highlights of Semana Santa. Continuing down Calle Santa Clara, and then right up Calle Santa Ana, you reach the **Alameda de Hércules**. This long avenue lined with planes and poplars is the centre of Sevilla's alternative scene. Once a marsh, it was drained in the 16th century and adorned at both ends with Roman columns; upon the taller of the two were placed sculptures of Hercules, who is said to have founded Sevilla, and Julius Caesar, whose presence as governor of the province is considerably more certain. On Sunday mornings (and a little on Thursdays), there's a lively flea market here; while Sevilla's busiest and oldest market, El Jueves, takes place on Thursday mornings too, a couple of blocks away on Calle Feria, which is named after it.

From the Alameda, follow Calle Peral, and then turn right up Calle Bécquer. This will bring you to the **Basílica de la Macarena** ⓘ *C Bécquer 1, T954-370195, daily 0900-1400, 1700-2100 (Semana Santa 0900-1500 most days), free (€5 for museum)*, the home of Sevilla's most-adored Mary and a fairly recent construction; the first stone was laid by Pope Pius XII in the 1940s. The Virgin takes pride of place in the *retablo*; the Christ from the other *paso* stands in front of her. You can see the *pasos* themselves in the museum, along with various gifts that have been bestowed on the Virgin and a variety of her garments.

Across the main road from the basilica is the **Hospital de las Cinco Llagas**. Built in the 16th century, it is said to have been the biggest hospital in the world at the time. The sober façade is long and impressive but these days the patients have been replaced by politicians; it's the seat of Andalucía's regional parliament. On the main road here begins the best-preserved stretch of the city walls. They were originally at least partially Roman, perhaps built by Julius Caesar when he governed the region. The Moors made them formidable again; with the circumference of some 6 km defended by 166 towers, a moat and jagged castellation.

Back at the basilica, take Calle San Luis, which meanders its way back towards the centre of town. You soon pass **Plaza del Pumarejo**, a shady spot frequented by some real barrio characters, then the **Iglesia de Santa Marina**, with a *mudéjar* tower. Shortly afterwards, on the right you come to the **Iglesia de San Luis** ⓘ *C San Luis s/n, T954-214024, Tue-Sat 0900-1400, Fri and Sat also 1700-2000, closed Aug, free*, whose flamboyant façade will snap you out of any heat-induced reverie. Although the road's too narrow to really appreciate the architecture, the front is a Baroque masterpiece with scores of Churrigueresque features. Inside the circular interior are several *retablos*, the finest is the main one, inlaid with blue ceramic and centred around a small Madonna painting; look out also for the massive Zurbarán painting depicting the saint Louis XIV of France in his earthly days. The ceiling frescoes in the dome are also very impressive; an ornate mirror is on hand to help you appreciate them.

Further down the street, the **Iglesia de San Marcos** is a Gothic-*mudéjar* church that was once a mosque. It has a well-crafted façade, with a toothed Gothic portal, delicate *mudéjar* blind arcading above, and the bearded evangelist himself atop. However, it is most notable for its slim tower, which is very similar in style to the Giralda. It's adorned with attractive brickwork and a series of windows that increase in size as the tower rises. Cervantes was fond of climbing to the top. The interior features some horseshoe arches, preserved despite extensive Civil War damage.

Behind the church, along Calle Santa Paula, is the **convent** ① *C Santa Paula s/n, T954-536330, Tue-Sun 1000-1300, €3*, of the same name. There's an air of mystery about a visit here; knock at the door and you'll eventually be admitted and get shown around by a knowledgeable old nun with a twinkle in her eye. It's the home of a few dozen nuns; the building dates from the 15th century and contains many pieces of art of varying quality and some fine faded, but wholly original, 15th-century *artesonado* ceilings. There's a gorgeous patio and a fine tiled doorway, a work of Pisano. On either side of the church is a pair of excellent sculptures by Martínez Montañés of the two Johns, while some Alonso Cano works are also present. Don't forget to buy some of the delicious marmalade made by the nuns.

## La Cartuja
the city's contemporary art gallery and a theme park

The clay-rich Isla de la Cartuja was a centre for potters' workshops in bygone centuries but was more or less derelict until the city decided to make it the site of the World Expo in 1992. Predictably for such an event, costs skyrocketed, and the city was left with massive debts and a huge space filled with modern buildings that needed to be used. There's a popular theme park here, Isla Mágica; nearby the river is spanned by two bridges by the Valencian architect Santiago Calatrava.

### Monasterio de la Cartuja
*Av Américo Vespucio 2, www.caac.es, Isla de la Cartuja, T955-037070. Tue-Sat 1100-2100, Sun 1100-1500. €1.80 for permanent collection or exhibition, €3 for both, free from 1900 weekdays and all day Sat; audio guide €3.*

The clay in this part of Sevilla meant that ceramics were made here from ancient times; it was in a pottery in the 13th century that the Virgin appeared and a shrine was built. It later became this important monastery, a favourite of Sevilla's wealthy and powerful in the Golden Age. Columbus came here to pray and contemplate his next voyages; when he died his remains lay here for 23 years.

In the Peninsular War, the arch-desecrator of Spanish cultural heritage, Maréchal Soult, stationed some troops here, and the buildings were badly damaged. Once the monks were expelled some 20 years later, it was in an extremely poor state and was picked up cheaply by Charles Pickman, a British businessman, who set up a ceramics factory on the site and lived there. Pickman generally respected the monastic buildings, though all were put to use, and the huge brick kilns and chimneys still dominate the site.

Renovated by the Sevillian authorities, it became the Royal Pavilion of Expo 92, and now houses a good contemporary art museum, the **Centro Andaluz de Arte Contemporáneo**. First visit the church itself, with a small cloister, a refectory with a beautiful coffered ceiling, and the well-carved tombs of the powerful Ribera family. Then access the galleries (the layout of the complex is confusing). The temporary exhibitions are usually good and the gallery spaces white, uncluttered, and relaxing.

The permanent collection (not all of which is always on display) has some excellent pieces, mostly by Andalucían artists. Look out for Guillermo Pérez Villalta's series on the four elements, which speaks powerfully about the fate of the Moors and their cultural contribution to Andalucía.

## Itálica and Alcalá de Guadaira

Roman ruins and a 14th-century monastery

### ★ Itálica

*Santiponce (9 km from Sevilla), T955-996583. Mid-Sep to Mar Tue-Sat 1000-1830, Sun 1000-1700, Apr to mid-Jun Tue-Sat 1000-2030, Sun 1000-1700, mid-Jun to mid-Sep Tue-Sat 1000-1700, Sun 1000-1700. Free EU citizens, otherwise €1.50. To get there, take the Damas (www.damas-sa.es) bus from Plaza de Armas bus station to Santiponce, €1.20 each way (25 mins), every 20-30 mins weekdays and on Sat mornings, every hour on Sat afternoons and Sun, by car take the N630 north (following the signposts for Mérida) across the Puente Cristo de la Expiración.*

It's hard to believe, wandering around the ruins of Itálica, that this was once one of the Roman Empire's largest and most important cities. In truth, little of it has been excavated; what you can walk around today is the partially revealed remains of the *nova urbs* (new town; a relative term these days), built by Hadrian in the early second century AD, while the *vetus urbs* (old town) lies under the village of Santiponce. It was originally built by Publius Cornelius Scipio in 206 BC; one of the Italian (not Roman) regiments of his army had a rough time of it during the battle against the Carthaginians at Illipa and he decided to build a settlement for them to let them heal up and ease the threat of mutiny. It grew rapidly and in time became the most important Roman city in the region, birthplace of the emperor Trajan and perhaps his protégé Hadrian, who certainly grew up here.

While it's a pleasant place to wander around, with birds, bees and acres of flowering weeds, there's not a huge amount to see (and the information given is paltry), but what's here is very good, particularly the huge amphitheatre near the entrance, which seated 20,000. Although much of the seating has been removed over the years, the terraces are still very clear, as are the stairways and the large sunken area in the middle (thought to have had a central dais erected over it for use in gladiatorial combats). One fascinating find is displayed in a side chamber: a bronze tablet inscribed with norms for gladiatorial combat imposed by Marcus Aurelius and his son (who else but Commodus, Russell Crowe's sworn enemy in *Gladiator*).

The other highlights of a visit are the mosaics on display on the floors of some of the excavated houses. The **House of Neptune** has one of these; the centre features sea creatures, including the god himself, while the outer edges depict a Nilotic hunting scene; it's not without its humour, as the large crane doing an injury to a hunter's backside attests. There's a statue of the god-emperor Trajan near here; it's thought that the whole of this section of the city was built by Hadrian in his predecessor's honour. The **House of the Birds** also has some excellent mosaics, two of which colourfully feature an array of the feathered tribe. The **House of the Planetarium** has perhaps the finest piece, with portraits of the seven divinities who gave their name to the Roman week.

It's hot out here, and there's not much shade, but thankfully there are several good bars and restaurants clustered around the entrance. If you're not exhausted yet, turn right out of the entrance and up the hill a couple of minutes to check out the partially restored Roman theatre (there's a tourist information point here). Don't bother with the small bathhouse nearby, but head straight for the monastery further up the road. The return bus passes the entrance to this, so you won't have to retrace your steps.

The **Monasterio San Isidoro del Campo** ⓘ *T955-998028, Wed-Thu 1000-1400, Fri-Sat 1000-1400, 1600-1900 (1700-2030 summer), Sun 1000-1500, €3*, was founded in 1301 by Guzmán El Bueno in the place where, by tradition, San Isidoro (StIsidore) had been interred until the removal of his remains to León. It's a sizeable monastery whose imposing walls attest to its double function as a fortress in those uncertain times. The place has had an interesting history; one of its monastic communities dabbled in translations of forbidden texts, not a healthy move in 16th century Spain with the Inquisition at the peak of its power and paranoia about Protestantism rife. Some of the monks fled the country, others burned for their bookish crimes. Guzmán and his wife are buried in the curious twin church, alongside a magnificent *retablo* by Martínez Montañés. One of the cloisters features unusual *mudéjar* frescoes.

## Alcalá de Guadaira

Now basically a suburb of Sevilla, the friendly village of Alcalá is worth visiting for its huge, muscular Moorish fortress, constructed by the Almohads. It's very impressive, if a shell; little remains inside the walls. Buses run every 20 minutes from Avenida Portugal (after 2100 they run from Prado San Sebastián bus station); €1.20.

## Tourist information

**Junta de Andalucía tourist office**
*Plaza del Triunfo, T954-221005, www. turismosevilla.org. Mon-Fri 0900-1930, Sat and Sun 0930-1930.*
Near the cathedral, Sevilla's most useful tourist office is always busy, but has good information and multilingual staff. Their former location on Av de la Constitución still resembles a tourist office but is actually a private business. There are also information booths at the airport and at platform 6 at Santa Justa train station. The tourist office sells the Sevilla Card for access to most museums and monuments, as well as free tour buses, river cruises, entry to the Isla Mágica theme park and discounts on flamenco shows. For a little extra it includes public transport. It costs €33 for 24 hrs or €53 for 48 hrs, slightly less online at www.sevillacard.es.

## Where to stay

There's a wealth of choice of attractive and intimate lodgings set in attractively renovated old Sevillian mansions. The densest concentration can be found in Barrio Santa Cruz and in San Vicente, between the Plaza de Armas bus station and the Museo de Bellas Artes.

If you're planning a visit in spring, booking ahead is advisable. All places raise their prices massively during Semana Santa and Feria; sometimes double or more, although it's more commonly 50-70%. At some hotels, this increase is in place for the whole Mar-May period. Price codes here reflect high season (but not Semana Santa) prices.

At many hotels you can get good discounts online rather than reserving with the hotel directly.

### The cathedral and around

**€€€€ Alfonso XIII**
*C San Fernando 2, T954-917000, www. hotel-alfonsoxiii-sevilla.com.*
One of Spain's most luxurious hotels, this huge neo-Moorish building was erected for the 1929 exhibition. Completely renovated recently, it's beautifully decorated with opulent patios. The hotel is 5-star in every sense of the word, but the prices are exorbitant at around €400-500 for a double, more during Sevilla's festive season. You'll get the best deals via the website.

**€€€€ Eme Catedral Hotel**
*C Alemanes 27, T954-560000, www. emecatedralhotel.com.*
This fashion-conscious modern hotel by the cathedral has brought a splash of colour and modern design to Sevilla's old centre. Certain humorous touches, undeniably attractive furnishings, and enticing features like the small rooftop pool and jacuzzi win it points; the rooms are stylish but perhaps lack features for this price. The location is wonderful.

**€€€ Hotel Alminar**
*C Alvarez Quintero 52, T954-293913, www.hotelalminar.com.*
On this likeable pedestrian street linking the cathedral with Plaza del Salvador, this hotel trades in warm personal service; with only 11 rooms, it feels like they've got time for all their guests. The rooms are spacious, modern, and

sparklingly clean, with efficient a/c and really good bathrooms. There's no parking particularly close.

### € TOC Hostel Sevilla
*T954-501244, Miguel Mañara 18, www. tocsevilla.com.*
It's hard to find fault with this brilliant spot slap-bang in the heart of the main monument area. It's got both private en suite rooms and comfortable dorms, all with upbeat modern decor and thoughtful design features. There's good security and staff have a helpful attitude. Great features include the reception desk and the back terrace. Recommended.

---

### Barrio Santa Cruz

### €€€€ Casa del Poeta
*C Don Carlos Alonso Chaparro 3, T954-213868, www.casadelpoeta.es.*
With a very discreet entrance in the heart of Santa Cruz (the street is a little cul-de-sac off Ximénez Enciso), this is another heart-stoppingly beautiful Sevilla patio hotel. Rooms are elegant and unfussily handsome – we loved the duplex one – and staff are professional and eager to please. Recommended.

### €€€€ Corral del Rey
*Corral del Rey 12, T954-227116, www. corraldelrey.com.*
This boutique hotel has turned heads in the Spanish hotel world for its faultlessly realized restoration of an historic *palacio*, its irresistible romantic ambience, thoughtfully selected modern art, and its beautiful rooms, which are coupled with excellent bathrooms and equipped with all sorts of amenities. There's a gourmet restaurant here, and a small rooftop pool; the staff are commendably solicitous. Recommended.

### €€€€ Las Casas de la Judería
*Callejón Dos Hermanas 7, T954-415150, www.casasypalacios.com.*
It's difficult to describe just how big this outstanding hotel complex is. It spreads across several old *palacios* in the Barrio Santa Cruz – all have been superbly renovated, with sparkling patios, pretty nooks, and hanging foliage. The rooms are sizeable, luxurious enough and agreeable, though not a patch on the exterior decor and a little dark and stuffy. Service is conscientious and there's live music in the piano bar every evening. A particular highlight of the hotel is the originally decorated underground passageway to the dining room. Recommended.

### €€€ El Rey Moro
*C Lope de Rueda 14, T954-563468, www. elreymoro.com.*
Run by the restaurant of the same name, this excellent hotel that sits between 2 central Santa Cruz streets is built around a large 3-storey patio with wooden columns. The appealing rooms have beams, big beds and shiny modern bathrooms; some face inwards on to the patio, others face the street and the buzz of the Plaza de los Venerables restaurants. Staff are charming, and rent out Segways to explore town. Breakfast included.

### €€ Hotel Amadeus & La Música
*C Farnesio 6, T954-501443, www. hotelamadeussevilla.com.*
A fantastic and original hotel occupying 2 adjacent buildings with a musical theme. The individually decorated rooms are named after composers; some have a piano, of which there are also a couple downstairs. All rooms have first-rate facilities. A highlight, apart from the charming service, is the spacious roof terrace with views

over the centre, including the Giralda. Highly recommended.

### €€ Hotel Goya
*C Mateos Gago 31, T954-211170, www. hotelgoyasevilla.com.*
Located at the top of the street that is Sevilla's tapas epicentre, the Goya is a cool place with marbled floors and a/c. The rooms are large and fairly minimalist, with excellent bathrooms. Some have balconies overlooking this interesting street.

### € Pensión San Pancracio
*Plaza de las Cruces 9, T954-413104, pensionsanpancracio@hotmail.com.*
In a quiet nook of the barrio, this is a good cheap choice; a touch faded, but well-scrubbed and quiet. There are several room choices: they are all adequate, with attractive white calico bedspreads and light and air from a central patio. The bathrooms are shared and clean. Ground floor rooms are cooler, but those above have a fan; take your pick.

### Self-catering
There's an ever-growing number of apartments around Barrio Santa Cruz; lots of them are listed online on sites like www.booking.com and www.airbnb.com.

### €€ Apartamentos Murillo
*C Reinoso 6, T954-216095, www. hotelmurillo.com.*
The **Hotel Murillo** in the heart of Santa Cruz also runs these stylish modern apartments around the corner. There are 3 types, sleeping up to 5, and fitted out with kitchen, bathroom, TV and phone. Rates are reasonable for this location. Also rented on a daily basis.

### Triana

### €€ Hotel Monte Triana
*C Clara de Jesús Montero 24, T954-343111, www.hotelesmonte.com.*
With a barrio location in Triana but close to the bus station and bridge, this makes an appealing and somewhat secluded Sevilla base. Staff are excellent and the modern rooms are very well kept. The buffet breakfast is better than average too.

### € Triana Backpackers
*C Rodrigo de Triana 69, T954-459960, www.trianabackpackers.com.*
This backpackers' hostel stands out for its Triana location as well as traveller-friendly features such as free internet, breakfast, a roof terrace and a TV lounge. It's a sociable place with friendly staff and a welcoming feel. It's not the cheapest, and couples won't get value from the cramped doubles, but it's a great place to meet other folk.

### El Arenal

### €€€ Hotel Adriano
*C Adriano 12, T954-293800, www. adrianohotel.com.*
This boutique hotel has a great location near the bullring and in the heart of a great tapas and restaurant area. Decor is in keeping with the building's 18th-century origins, with antique furniture and gilt trim. There's parking available too; another pleasing feature.

### €€ Hotel Simón
*C García de Vinuesa 19, T954-226660, www.hotelsimonsevilla.com.*
Long a Sevilla favourite, this is an attractive hotel built around a beautiful airy courtyard with a fountain. There are plenty of azulejos and neo-Moorish features. Rooms are smallish

but accommodating and decorated as thoughtfully as the rest of the establishment. It's not luxurious, but good value for the decor and ambience.

## Centro and San Vicente

**€€€€ Las Casas del Rey de Baeza**
*Plaza Jesús de la Redención 2, off C Santiago, T954-561496, www.hospes.com.*
An enchanting place to stay near Casa de Pilatos, this old *corral de vecinos* has been superbly restored to be charming but not overdone. The patios are surrounded by pretty wooden galleries and the underfloor hessian mats are a great touch. The rooms are big, with huge beds and all facilities. Guests have use of a rooftop pool and terrace as well as an elegantly decorated library and lounges. The service is first rate. Recommended.

**€€€ Las Casas de los Mercaderes**
*C Alvarez Quintero 9, T954-136211, www. aahoteles.com.*
In the heart of the shopping district and a short walk from the centre is this beautifully renovated hotel. The tempting rooms are interestingly furnished and spacious, with all conveniences; the hotel is built around a striking arcaded patio. Elegant 19th-century furnishings in the public areas complete the classy but welcoming feeling.

**€€ Pensión Virgen de la Luz**
*C Virgen de la Luz 18, T954-537963, www. pensionvirgendelaluz.es.*
One of Sevilla's best-value cheapies, this pretty little place is near the Casa de Pilatos. The rooms come with or without bath; the latter (**€**) are of an unusually high standard and represent good value, particularly those on the lane, which have a small plant-filled balcony. The beds are welcoming, the bathroom spotless, and the patio decorated caringly with blue tiling.

**€ Hostal Museo**
*C Abad Gordillo 17, T954-915526, www. hostalmuseo.com.*
Offering excellent value for money, this clean and courteously run place is a short stroll from the bus station and very close to the art gallery. There are flawless, comfortable rooms, as well as a lift, not seen in many Sevilla *hostales*.

## Self-catering

**Sevilla Apartamentos**
*T667-511348, www.sevillapartamentos. com.*
This organization has well-furnished apartments for short-term rental in different areas of Sevilla. Prices start at €266 for 2 people per week, which is very good value.

## La Macarena

The Macarena barrio, particularly around the Alameda de Hércules, is a great spot to be based if you want to explore the untouristy parts of old Sevilla; there are great tapas and nightlife and no camera-toting hordes.

**€€€ Hotel Alcoba del Rey**
*C Bécquer 9, T954-915800, www. alcobadelrey.com.*
Close to the home of the Virgen de Macarena, this comfortable hotel offers cordial service and plentiful facilities at the western edge of the old town. The decor is Moroccan-inspired, with attractive imported furniture lending a North African ambience. Every room is stylish and distinct, with unusual bathroom arrangements providing plenty of romance and charm. The best of the rooms has a candlelit jacuzzi; a honeymoon special.

### €€€ Patio de la Alameda
*Alameda de Hércules 56, T954-904999, www.patiodelaalameda.com.*
This classy apartment hotel makes a top-value place to stay. Built around a striking orange restored patio, it has excellent rooms with sitting room, kitchen and all facilities. The location right on the Alameda de Hércules is great for strolling and bar-hopping. Recommended.

### €€€ Sacristía Santa Ana Hotel
*Alameda de Hércules 22, T954-915722, www.hotelsacristia.com.*
This boutique hotel is a sensitive and sumptuous conversion of a noble 18th-century mansion in a most appealing Macarena location. It's built around an elegant patio and has warm, personal service. The rooms have a classical ambience, with ornate headboards and tiled floors; you'll get some night noise at weekends from the ones at the front. There's also a restaurant. Recommended.

### € Hostal Macarena
*C San Luis 91, T954-370141, www. hostalmacarenasevilla.com.*
Great budget option on Plaza del Pumarejo; friendly, family run and set around a lovely atrium, with beautiful tilework and attractive furniture. Rooms come with or without bath.

## Restaurants

There's little distinction between restaurants and tapas bars in Sevilla; most restaurants include an area to stand and snack, while at tapas bars you can usually sit down and order meal-sized portions (*raciones*). Accepted practice is to stand at the bar, have a couple of tapas and also taste what your friends are eating. A standard tapa will cost €2.50-5. Tapas portions and set menus virtually disappear during Semana Santa when restaurants and bars are full to bursting.

Most central restaurants offer traditional Sevilla cuisine; if you fancy finer dining, head out to the new town, where upmarket restaurants congregate around avenues like Eduardo Dato.

### The cathedral and around

### €€ Ovejas Negras
*C Hernando Colón 8, T955 123811, www. ovejasnegrastapas.com.*
Just around the corner from the cathedral but packed with locals as well as visitors, this buzzy modern bar keeps the quality high and the atmosphere relaxed. Fusion flavour combinations make for some stellar tapas plates, which are very generously proportioned. Wines are excellent also. Recommended.

### Barrio Santa Cruz
The lovely Barrio Santa Cruz is an obvious place to eat, with its shady plazas and terraces. Unfortunately, a high percentage of the restaurants are aimed at tourists, and serve below-par food at inflated prices.

### €€ Carmela
*C Santa María la Blanca 6, T954-531432.*
From 0900 onwards. One of the better of the terraced bars on this long plaza, Carmela serves good breakfasts, plenty of vegetarian dishes and snacks, and decent tapas (top gazpacho), as well as a *plato del día* that's good value for this area. It's also available at night.

### €€ Las Teresas
*C Santa Teresa 2, T954-213069.*
Research indicates that 9 out of 10 people dredge up an image very

similar to this Santa Cruz local when they think the words 'tapas bar'. Hams: check, tiles: check, patina of age: check, gruff but lovable bar staff: check, mouth-watering smell of fried fish: check. Popular with locals and visitors. Recommended.

### €€ Taberna Poncio
*C Ximénez de Enciso 33, T954 460717, www.ponciorestaurantes.com.*
Sashimi, ravioli or succulent pork medallions might come your way at this worthwhile Santa Cruz tapas restaurant. Eschew the high tables in the foyer for the more relaxing dining room or bench-top eating in the bar. Service is correct, and some dishes hit real heights. Portions are generous; 2 tapas per person is ample.

### € Bar Alfalfa
*Corner C Alfalfa and C Candilejo, T654-809297.*
On the square of the same name, this excellent Italian tapas bar is decorated with farming implements, earthenware jars and hundreds of bottles of wine. Enjoy a perfect *bruschetta* here, divine *bresaola* or a selection of Italian cheeses. You can order streetside on warm evenings. Recommended.

### € Bodega Santa Cruz
*C Rodrigo Caro 2, T954-213246.*
This busy and cheerful bar does some of Sevilla's choicest tapas and *montaditos*, with *cazón en adobo* or *pringá* particularly delicious. As the night wears on, the frantically busy bar staff wipe what they've run out of off the menus, which are chalked up at each end of the bar. Sees plenty of tourists but still very authentic. Also known as **Las Columnas**. Recommended.

### € La Goleta
*C Mateos Gago 22, T954-218966.*
Simple, tiny bar with loads of atmosphere. Run by a notable local character, it's an historic Santa Cruz watering hole. It specializes in a tasty orange wine; the tapas are limited but excellent. Humorous touches abound, and when the boss Alvaro's on form it's a one-man show. There's a more spacious extension open next door but the original is best.

## Triana
C Betis that runs along the river is full of places to eat and drink, not all of them good. C San Jacinto is pedestrianized and has some reliably excellent options.

### €€€ Abades Triana
*C Betis 69, T954-286459, www. abadestriana.com.*
A comparatively recent arrival to the riverbank in Triana, this restaurant occupies a hard-to-miss modern building that's all glass and light, offering wonderful views over the Guadalquivir and across to the old town. The food is high-priced, but there are some very tasty fish dishes and an inventive tapas degustation menu. The location is especially seductive at night.

### €€ La Blanca Paloma
*C Pagés del Corro 86, T954-333788.*
This cheerful Triana venue was always one of the best tapas stops this side of the Guadalquivir. It has the same boisterous bar scene and also offers an excellent restaurant, with the same philosophy of originality combined with good humour and high-quality ingredients. Try the *bacalao al horno* (baked cod with a prawn sauce).

### € Taberna Miami
*C San Jacinto 21, T954-340843.*
A stalwart tapas bar with many tempting offers, decorated with photos of pilgrimages to Rocío and Santiago, as well as a couple of boars' heads. Portions are very generous; 2 tapas and you'll feel like you've had dinner. It's a cheery spot to be and is great value. Recommended.

## El Arenal

### €€ Bodega Antonio Romero
*C Antonia Díaz 19, T954-223939.*
Cheery waistcoated waiters man the bar at this warm and inviting venue. It's got a very typical feel, and serves up delicious tapas like grilled goat's cheese, as well as staples like thick tortilla and well-cut ham. There are several offshoots nearby.

### €€ Enrique Becerra
*C Gamazo 2, T954-213049.*
A fabulous, traditional tapas bar and restaurant serving reliably excellent Andalucían specialities in pretty dining areas with rustic painted wooden furniture. The swordfish in amontillado sherry is especially good, but so is everything else, including an impressive wine list.

### €€ Horacio Restaurante
*Antonia Díaz 9, T954-225385.*
On a street that's impressively stocked with quality eating choice, this has plenty to recommend it. Decorated with still-life canvases and soft yellow walls, it offers excellent, and fairly priced dishes – the grilled vegetables, avocado, prawn and walnut salad, and tossed tuna in soy sauce all impress – alongside warm service and decent wines.

### €€ La Brunilda
*C Galera 5, T954 220481, www.facebook. com/labrunilda.*
Exposed brick and a backstreet location give this a romantic feel ... or they would, if it weren't the latest trendy Sevilla bar on the food hound circuit. The tapas are great, featuring fresh market produce with refreshing twists, but expect to queue: not just for a table, but even to get to the bar.

### €€ La Bulla
*C Dos de Mayo 26, T954-219262, www. facebook.com/labulla.*
Reader-recommended, this buzzy modern tavern offers high-quality tapas, with beautiful presentation and great originality, all at a very fair price. Staff are helpful.

### € Bar Pepe Hillo
*C Adriano 24, T954-215390.*
A legend in its own tapas-time, this place is always full to bursting with animated *sevillanos* enjoying their tasty stews and *croquetas* among other goodies. A pork *solomillo* in sweet wine and raisin sauce is another star. High ceilinged, busy and buzzy, it's decorated with farming implements and no fewer than 10 bulls' heads lugubriously observe proceedings. There's a very attractive dining area out the back, away from the hurly-burly of the bar.

### € Casa Morales
*C García de Vinuesa 11, T954-221242.*
This great old place is in a one-time sherry bodega – the big jars in one of the 2 bars used to hold the stuff. The service is old style, with orders scrawled on serviettes and friendly chat. The tapas and *montaditos* are served on a wee wooden tray; the *guiso del día* (stew of the day) is often a tempting option. Recommended.

## Centro and San Vicente

### €€€ Taberna del Alabardero
*C Zaragoza 20, T954-502721, www.*
*tabernadelalabardero.es.*
This hospitality school is also one of the
city's best restaurants. It's pricey but
worth it; the menu changes seasonally,
but look out for house specials such
as *corvina* (sea bass) with spinach,
kidneys and grapes, or succulent beef
fillet with blue *cabrales* cheese. There's
a good-value *menú de degustación* for
€65. For cheaper eats or a coffee, stay
downstairs and head to the back, where
*raciones* and *montaditos* are served. The
building was once home of the Sevillian
poet Covestany and also has a handful of
well-appointed rooms available (€€€).

### €€ Casa la Viuda
*C Albareda 2, T954-215420, www.*
*comerdetapasensevilla.es.*
There's a thriving tapas scene in
the streets north of the town hall at
lunchtimes, where tourists and civil
servants rub shoulders in a variety of bars.
This is perhaps the best, with delicious
and generously proportioned tapas at fair
prices. They are innovative and beautifully
presented, but it's not modern cuisine:
think lots of sauces, spices and garlic. They
offer interesting wines too.

### € El Rinconcillo
*C Gerona 40, T954-223183, www.*
*elrinconcillo.es.*
An incredibly old bar that was
founded in 1670 when the large-jawed
Habsburgs still ruled Spain. It's an
attractive place that's definitely worth a
visit. The fittings are all wooden and the
hams hanging over the counter look to
be as old as the bar. The tapas are good
and served until fairly late; the *croquetas*
are particularly memorable.

### € La Antigua Bodeguita
*Plaza del Salvador 6, T954-561833.*
As long as the weather holds, the interior
of this popular bar is just a place to order,
as the crowd from here and the bar next
door spills out on to the square. It's a
great Sevillian scene in its own right, but
the tapas are also worthy, particularly the
seafood. Check out *mojama*, cured tuna
meat, which will either delight or disgust.

## Cafés

### La Campana
*C Sierpes 1, T954-223570.*
An institution in this part of town, this
place will seduce the sweet-toothed
with its ice creams and pastries. During
Semana Santa, when it's *the* place to
have a seat booked, it has an impressive
display of pointy caramel *nazarenos*. At
other times, try the *yemas* or the *lenguas
de almendra*.

## La Macarena

### €€ Yebra
*C Medalla Milagrosa 3, T954-351007,*
*www.yebrarestauracion.com. Closed Mon.*
Just outside the walls beyond the
edge of Macarena barrio, this is one of
Sevilla's best tapas joints; a smart but
relaxed place offering authentic and
original gourmet tapas at around €3-4.
It's not often that you'll see partridge or
pheasant on tapas menus, but you do
here. The only drawback is its popularity;
getting an order in can be a nightmare.

### € Cervecería Yerbabuena
*C Feria s/n.*
The Macarena barrio has a real
community feel to it, and there's
nowhere better to experience it than
in its picturesque food market. On Sat,
locals and stallholders mingle at this bar

at the corner of the market, enjoying a cold beer and tapa in the sunshine.

## Bars and clubs

Sevilla's nightlife can't compete in terms of variety with Barcelona or Madrid, but you certainly won't be left sipping vodka in an empty bar. Sevilla folk tend to call it a night fairly early midweek and party until sun-up come the weekend, but there are plenty of zones that are always lively, particularly around Plaza Alfalfa in the old town and C Betis in Triana; both populated by a mixture of locals and tourists. The Viapol zone in the new town Nervión has a much more local scene, with heaps of bars and *discotecas*, and the character-packed Alameda de Hércules buzzes with a fairly alternative set.

### Bars

#### Bulebar Café
*Alameda de Hércules 83, T954-294212, www.cafebulebar.com.*
One of several good choices on this long promenade, the **Bulebar** is colourfully decorated and has a great terrace. It's a popular meeting point for an alternative set and has a relaxed feel about it.

#### Kiosco del Agua
*Paseo de Colón 10, www.facebook.com/ kioscodelagua.*
On the riverfront across the road from the Teatro Maestranza, this is one of Sevilla's best spots for an evening beer. Sit on the wrought-metal chairs and watch the sun set over Triana while bats and swallows flutter among the silhouetted palm trees. Good views of the floodlit Torre del Oro too.

#### Puerto de Cuba
*C Betis s/n, www.puertodecubasevilla. com. Fri-Sun from 1700, daily at busy times.*
It's hard to imagine a more romantic location than this garden bar right on the river below the **Abades** restaurant in Triana. Torchlight, designer couches, and palm fronds make this feel like an enclave of the Caribbean by the Guadalquivir; it's the perfect place for a stylish evening drink.

#### The Second Room
*C Placentines 19, T603-628759, www. facebook.com/TheSecondRoom. Open 1500-0200 or 0300.*
Great *copas*, cocktails and mojitos served by waiting staff who don't seem to have the usual attitude problem – in fact, they look pleased to be here. Top views of the Giralda.

### Clubs

#### Antique Theatro
*C Matemáticos Rey Pastor y Castro s/n, T954-462207, www.antiquetheatro.com. Daily Jun-Sep, Wed-Sun the rest of the year. Open 2400-0700, but don't turn up until at least 0300 unless you want the place to yourself. Cover charge €10-15 with a drink.*
Sevilla's most upmarket nightclub, with an excellent sound system and committed DJs in one of the old pavilions from the 1992 Expo.

#### Fun Club
*Alameda de Hércules 84, T636-669023, www.funclubsevilla.com. Thu-Sat 2400-0600 or so. Entry is around €5 or often free otherwise.*
A music venue and *discoteca* with some serious alternative cred in these parts. There's often live rock, drum 'n' bass or good DJs.

### Groucho
*C Federico Sánchez Bedoya 22, T954-216039, www.grouchobar.com. Entry €10 including a drink.*
This stylish *discoteca* is tucked away on an Arenal side street and is definitely one of the city's in spots to be seen. There are 3 rooms and 2 dance floors; be prepared to queue at weekends.

### Itaca
*C Amor de Dios 31, www.facebook.com/itacadisco.*
Sevilla's best-established gay *discoteca*, always well attended, and with appropriately good dance music. There's a backroom and shows from Wed-Sat nights.

## Entertainment
Your best guide to upcoming events is the magazine *El Giraldillo*, www.elgiraldillo.es. *Cultura en Sevilla* is another free publication worth checking out for cultural events.

### Cinema
Check www.ecartelera.com/cartelera for what's on.
**Avenida**, *C Marqués de Paradas 15, T954-293025.* Original version films subtitled in Spanish.

### Flamenco
Whether you're planning to spend every hour of darkness trawling bars in search of the most authentic *cante jondo* or just want to briefly experience what it's all about, it's likely that you'll want to see some flamenco when you're in Sevilla. While much of what's on offer is geared to tourists (although frequently of a very high technical standard), it's still possible to track down a more authentic experience.

There are essentially 3 ways to see flamenco in Sevilla. The *tablaos* are organized performances in set venues, with entry ranging from €15-30. The crowd at these is mostly tourists, the performers often well known and of a very high standard, and the emotion factor usually low.

Secondly, there are many bars that have dedicated flamenco nights; the quality varies according to the artist and the atmosphere, the cost is minimal and occasionally you'll see something very special.

Thirdly, in bars where flamenco enthusiasts hang out – and there are still plenty in Triana – you may see some impromptu performances. The tourist office has a fuller list of shows and flamenco bars.

**Auditorio Alvarez Quintero**, *C Alvarez Quintero 48, T954-293949, www.alvarezquintero.com.* Daily evening shows at 2100 that are among the most authentic of the *tablaos*. €18 entry.

**Casa Anselma**, *C Pagés del Corro 49, Triana. Open 2000-0100.* A busy and beautifully decorated bar with free entry but expensive drinks. There's live music every night (except Sun when it's closed); it tends to be popular Sevilla ditties and *rocieras* (music associated with the pilgrimage to El Rocío in Huelva province) rather than pure flamenco, but it can be entertaining, particularly when Anselma herself is on form. At 2400 she belts out *Salve Rociera*.

**Casa de la Memoria**, *C Cuna 6, T954-029999, www.casadelamemoria.es.* 2 nightly shows of good quality at this venue in central Sevilla. They cost €18; this is good value, as the performers are usually excellent and the atmosphere intimate; be sure to book in advance as it's a small venue. You can book tickets at the Centro de Interpretación de la Judería in Barrio Santa Cruz too.

**La Carbonería**, *C Leviés 18, T954-214460, www.levies18.com. Open 2000-0330.* Long-established, popular sprawling bar, a former coal yard (hence the name) where flamenco is performed at 2330 every night. It's very touristy, but there's sometimes a strong gypsy presence too, and some of the flamenco is very good. There's also a tapas counter, a beer garden and a front bar. Free (but the drinks are slightly pricier than normal).

**Los Gallos**, *Plaza de Santa Cruz 11, Barrio Santa Cruz, T954-216981, www. tablaolosgallos.com.* This is a touristy *tablao* but definitely one of the best of its kind, with high-quality performers who don't seem to be going through the motions. There are 2 shows a night; go to the later one. €35 including a drink.

**Museo del Baile Flamenco**, *C Manuel Rojas Marcos 3, T954-340311, www. museoflamenco.com.* Live performances by good artists every night, €20, 2 shows nightly, ticket includes a guided walk through Santa Cruz, book ahead.

### Music
The main venues for classical concerts are the theatres (see below). For live music, see also Bars and clubs, above, and Flamenco, above. *El Giraldillo* is the best guide to upcoming performances.

### Theatre
These theatres put on a range of drama, music and dance.

**La Fundición**, *Casa de la Moneda, C Habana s/n, T954-225844, www. fundiciondesevilla.es.* In the attractively refurbished complex that was once the royal mint, this has a variety of comedy, flamenco, dance, and other theatre.

**Teatro Lope de Vega**, *Av María Luisa, T954-590867, www.teatrolopedevega.org.* This lovely building built for the 1929 exhibition has some excellent theatre and music at bargain prices; some tickets are only €5.

**Teatro Maestranza**, *Paseo de Cristóbal Colón, T954-223344, www. teatrodelamaestranza.es.* This acclaimed modern building is Sevilla's main venue for opera, drama and dance. The ticket office is open daily 1000-1400, 1800-2100; it's a fairly dressy scene.

### Festivals

It's well worth planning your trip to coincide with the solemn Semana Santa processions or the subsequent Feria de Abril, but you'll be paying more for accommodation and should reserve rooms well in advance.

**5 Jan Cabalgata de los Reyes Magos**, is a colourful night parade of the 3 kings through the streets. They travel in colourful carriages and toss sweets and gifts to onlookers.

**Easter Semana Santa** (29 Mar-5 Apr 2015, 20-27 Mar 2016, 9-16 Apr 2017, 23 Mar-1 Apr 2018). The most famous of Spain's celebrations is in Sevilla. Members of the city's 52 *cofradías* parade *pasos* of Christ and the Virgin through the city streets. See box, page 18.

**Apr Feria de Abril** is the major social event of the Sevilla calendar. Upwards of 1000 *casetas* (small pavilions) see a week of eating, drinking and parading their pretty horse carriages and *flamenca* dresses. See box, page 26.

**Sep** (even years only) **Bienal de Flamenco**, is a major flamenco event, held in various venues around the city. Check www.labienal.com for information.

**7 Dec Fiesta de la Inmaculada**, *tunas* (traditional student minstrel bands) gather at night in the Plaza del Triunfo to sing traditional songs. In the morning children perform the *Danza de los Seises* in the cathedral.

## Shopping

### Books
**Antonio Castro**, *C Sol 3, T954-217030, www.castrolibros.es.* Nice old second-hand bookshop in the old town with a respectable selection of English paperbacks.
**La Casa del Libro**, *C Velásquez 8, T954-502950, www.casadellibro.com.* Good large bookshop for any needs, including travel or English language.

### Ceramics
If it's superb ceramics you're after, Triana is the place to go; there are dozens of attractively decorated shops; many have been family run for generations. Most of these shops are used to tourists and can arrange reasonably priced secure international delivery. If you're not an EU resident, pick up an IVA-exemption form with any major purchase, see page 105.
**Cerámica Santa Ana**, *C San Jorge 31, T954-333990, www.ceramicasantaana. com.* One of a few excellent ceramic shops in this area.
**Pilar Márquez Pérez/Cerámica Aracena**, *C Sierpes 36, T954-215228.* A good place to buy Sevillian tiles and other painted ceramics. Some are hand painted in the shop itself, which can be good to watch.

### Clothes and fashion
Sevilla's main shopping zone is around **C Sierpes**, **C Tetuán**, **C Velásquez**, **C Cuna** and **Plaza del Duque**. This busy area is the place to come for clothes, be it well-priced modern Spanish gear, or essential Sevilla Feria fashion: shawls, *flamenca* dresses, ornamental combs, castanets and fans.

Head to the **Alameda de Hércules** area for more offbeat shopping, either in the lively markets, or the smaller shops along **C Amor de Dios**, **C Jesús del Gran Poder** or **C Trajano**.

### Department stores
**El Corte Inglés**, *Plaza del Duque 7 and 13, T954-220931, Av Luis Montoto 122, T954-571440, Plaza Magdalena 1, T954-218855, C San Pablo 1, T954-218855, www.elcorte ingles.es.* Spain's premier department store, with almost anything you could want to buy.

### Food and drink
**Baco**, *C Cuna 4, T902-211313, www. baco.es. Mon-Sat 0930-1430, 1700-2100.* Spanish and foreign products, good for classy picnic fare.

### Markets
Sevilla has some excellent street markets. A famous flea market takes place on Sun mornings in the **Alameda de Hércules**; there is a smaller one on Thu too. The big Thu event, **El Jueves**, takes place on nearby C Feria, when the whole street is filled with stalls of every description. **Plaza Alfalfa** has a curious Sun morning animal market. There are excellent food markets in **Triana** by the Puente Isabel II and in **La Macarena**, also on C Feria.

## What to do

### Bike hire
Bike stands are all over the centre, with a €13.33 weekly fee plus a small per-hire cost. See www.sevici.es (Spanish only) for details.

**Bici4City**, *C Peral 6, T954-229883, www.bici4city.com.* Rent bikes (€3 per hr, €15 for 24 hrs) and audio guides. Also have mountain bikes available and run guided tours.

**Rentabike**, *Pl Santa Cruz 4, T955-118228, www.rentabikesevilla.com.* Hires various types of bike (from €10 per day) and also has daily bike tours of the city.

### Bullfighting

Although controversial, bullfighting is very popular in Sevilla; Andalucía is really the cradle of *los toros*. Sevilla's bullring, **La Maestranza**, is the 2nd most prestigious in Spain and draws top fighters every year. Sevilla has around 28 bullfights a season, one every day in Feria, then every Sun until Sep. The highest standard can be seen at Feria and at the season's end, but you'll pay more for tickets, and they are harder to get hold of. For big fights, it's worth reserving several days in advance at the *taquilla* at the bullring, or at one of the agents on Puerta de Jerez or C Tetuán,

who add on a small commission. Or book at www.taquillatoros.com.

### Football

Sevilla's main sporting passion is football. While international matches, when they come to town, are mostly played at the Estadio Olímpico, the city's 2 main clubs, **Real Betis** and **Sevilla**, have their own stadiums. Going to a match can be a great experience; there's much more of a family atmosphere than in the majority of European countries. One of the 2 teams will be at home almost every weekend of the Spanish season. Games take place on Sat and Sun with one game on Mon evening. You can buy tickets at the grounds during business hours or before the match; they don't sell out unless they're playing Real Madrid, Barcelona or the volatile local derby.

Agencies on C Tetuán also sell tickets, for a small mark-up. Tickets are pricey, with the cheapest seats starting at about €25.

**Real Betis Balompié**, *Estadio Manuel Ruíz de Lopera, Av de la Palmera s/n, T954-610340, www.realbetisbalompie.es.* Traditionally representing the working class of the city, Betis play in green and white stripes. They have won the league only once, in 1935. In the second division at time of writing.

**Sevilla FC**, *Estadio Sánchez Pizjuan, Av Eduardo Dato s/n, T954-535353, www.sevillafc.es.* Play in white and red and won the league in 1946. In recent years have been one of the best teams outside the big two of Real Madrid and Barcelona.

### Tours

There are 2 identical **open-top bus tours** of the city, with the usual multilingual commentary. Both leave from the Torre

## Language schools

There's a huge number, and you're recommended to do lots of research. **Instituto de Estudios de la Lengua Española** (IELE), C García de Vinuesa 29, T954-560788, www.iele.com, is a popular school; **Lenguaviva**, C Viriato 24, T915-943776, www.lenguaviva.net, offers crash courses and longer options, various accommodation options and excursions; **CLIC**, C Albareda 19, T954-502131, www. clic.es, is a frequently recommended school with lively teaching, youngish students and packages including accommodation and excursions.

del Oro every 30 mins from 1000. They have the same stops and hop-on-hop-off system, free walking tour and 1992 Expo site tour. They cost €18 for a 24-hr ticket, but it's worth bargaining and checking for special promos.

For a cruise on the river, **Cruceros Turísticos Torre del Oro**, T954-561692, www.crucerostorredeloro.com, departs every 30 mins from 1100 to 2200 (1900 winter) from the quay by the Torre del Oro. It goes both ways along the river, and points out the sights, including the old quays where Magellan and others once set sail. Bar on board. €16, under-14s free, cruise lasts 1 hr. For a much more intimate experience, **Guadaluxe**, T661-278826, www.guadaluxe.com, offer personal cruises in a small boat, with a friendly skipper and good information on both sights and river wildlife.

There are several **walking tours** of Sevilla; contact the tourist information office for details. There are tapas tours, tours on bikes, walks in Triana, and guided visits to the cathedral and Alcázar. Try **Sevilla Walking Tours**, www.sevillawalkingtours.com.

**Horse carriages** can be found everywhere, particularly near the cathedral. Seating up to 5, they'll take you on a trot around the city; you can specify which things you want to see. Rates vary in season, and bargaining is useful; think €45-60 for a ride of 50 mins or so. Drivers provide a commentary of dubious accuracy.

### Watersports
**Pedalquivir**, *T679-194045, www. pedalquivir.com*. Rental of rowing boats, pedalos and canoes on the river near the bullring.

### Transport

#### Air
Sevilla's airport is 10 km northeast of the centre. A bus runs to central Sevilla (Prado de San Sebastián bus station) via the train station. It goes roughly every 30 mins Mon to Sat (hourly or better on Sun) and takes 30 mins (€4). A taxi to town costs a fixed €22.20 during the day, slightly more at night or weekends.

**Easyjet** and **Ryanair** connect Sevilla with several European cities including **London**, and there are many domestic routes run by **Iberia**, **Vueling** and others. For airport information, T954-449000.

#### Bus
The city of Sevilla is one of Spain's major destinations for interurban buses. They arrive at 2 stations, Plaza de Armas for destinations north and west, and Prado de San Sebastián for the south and east.

**Local** Sevilla's fleet of **TUSSAM** buses (T902-459954, www.tussam.es) provides a good service around the city. A single fare is €1.40 (drivers will give change up to a point), but you can buy a 1- or 3-day tourist card for €5/10 respectively. The most useful bus services are the circular routes: bus C5 does a tight circuit of the historic centre; buses C1 and C2 run via Santa Justa train station and the Expo site (C1 goes clockwise, C2 anti-clockwise); while C3 (clockwise) and C4 (anti-clockwise) follow the perimeter of the old walls, except for C3's brief detour into Triana. You can examine routes online, download a route map or pick up a map from the **TUSSAM** kiosk on Plaza Encarnación.

**Long distance** Sevilla has 2 principal bus stations. The larger, **Plaza de**

**Armas,** by the river near the Puente del Cachorro, T954-038655, www.autobusesplazadearmas.es, serves destinations to the north and the west of the city. These include **Madrid** (6 hrs, hourly), **Huelva** (½-hourly, 1 hr 15 mins via motorway, longer via main road) and 3 daily buses to **Asturias** via **Mérida**, **Cáceres** (these 2 are serviced hourly anyway), **Salamanca**, **Zamora** and **León**. There's a day and a night bus to **Lisbon** (6-8 hrs), remember that Portugal is 1 hr behind), and daily buses to **Faro** and **Lagos** in the Algarve. There are also buses to **Alicante**, **Valencia** and **Barcelona**.

The other bus station, **Prado de San Sebastián**, is near the Barrio Santa Cruz on Plaza San Sebastián, T954-417111. It serves destinations east and south of the city. There are buses almost hourly to **Jerez de la Frontera** and **Cádiz** (1 hr 30 mins), **Córdoba** (1 hr 45 mins), as well as **Granada** (7 daily, 3 hrs), **Jaén** and **Almería**. There are also connections to a number of smaller Andalucían towns.

For both bus stations, the biggest operators are **Alsa** (www.alsa.es) and **Damas** (www.damas-sa.es).

## Car

Sevilla isn't a great place to have a car due to the narrow one-way streets of the old town, lack of parking, high car crime and the confusing layout. There are plenty of underground car parks that cost about €3 per hr/€25 per day, and most hotels have a car park or access to one.

**Car hire** There are major international firms at the airport, including **Budget**, www.budget.com, T954-999137, and **Hertz**, T954-514720, www.hertz.com. **Avis**, T954-537861, www. avis.com, have an office at the train station.

## Motorcycle hire
**Vespasur,** C Júpiter 25, T954-417500, www. vespasur.es. Discounts for hire of 3 days or more. Near Santa Justa train station.

## Taxis
A ride right across town, for example from the cathedral to the Puerta de Macarena, or Triana to the train station, will cost €6-10. Prices rise slightly after 2200, at weekends and during fiestas such as Semana Santa or Feria. T954-622222 or T954-580000 to book.

## Train
Sevilla's modern train station, Santa Justa, is a 15-min walk from the centre on Av Kansas City.

For train information **RENFE** have a good telephone information line, T902-240202, and their website is www.renfe.com. There's a booking agent in the centre at C Zaragoza 29.

Sevilla is served by the high-speed AVE train, which cuts travel time to Madrid and Córdoba to impressively low levels. It's expensive, but a good option. If you travel *preferente* class, up to 50% more expensive, you get access to an a/c hospitality waiting room (free food and drinks). Groups can get a great deal booking a table for four in *preferente* class.

There are 10-15 daily trains to **Cádiz** (1 hr 45 mins-2 hrs), stopping at **Jerez** (1 hr). There are 3 daily trains to **Barcelona** (2 fast, 5½ hrs, 1 slow, 11 hrs), 1 to **Valencia** (8½ hrs) and lots of high-speed services to **Madrid** (up to 20 AVE fast trains daily, 2 hrs 25 mins). To **Córdoba**, there are 6 normal trains daily, 1 hr 20 mins; and up to 24 AVE trains, 41 mins.

Both fast and slow trains head for **Málaga** (2 hrs 40 mins/1 hr 55 mins). There are also trains to **Jaén**, **Huelva**, and **Granada**.

# Around
## Sevilla city

The bulk of Sevilla province is undulating farmland, and there's not a great deal of scenic interest. However, north from Sevilla are the low hills of the Sierra Morena, with lightly forested slopes and valleys making this a great walking destination.

A few small towns beckon through the heat haze east of Sevilla; Carmona with its excellent Roman graveyard, the spires of Ecija, and the elegant ducal seat of Osuna.

## Sierra Morena
gently rolling countryside, quiet and attractive towns and good walks

★North of Sevilla, the Sierra Morena is a popular weekend trip from the capital. The region's main town is Cazalla de la Sierra, while nearby Constantina is the base for the Parque Natural Sierra Norte, covering much of this part of the province. Heading west, you can cross into the fascinating Huelvan section of the Sierra Morena, home to Spain's finest ham.

### Cazalla de la Sierra
This pleasing whitewashed town is the most useful base for exploring the northern reaches of Sevilla's province. Once an Iberian settlement, it was controlled in turn by the Romans and the Moors, who named it thus (meaning fortified town). The town is now known for its production of *aguardiente*, including the much-imbibed *Miura* cherry-flavoured anis. The company has a shop in the centre of the village.

The town's church, **Nuestra Señora de la Consolación**, is worth a look; massive in scale, it's a real mixture of styles, with a keep-like main section featuring layered brick and stone walls; this is *mudéjar* and dates from the 14th-15th centuries, as does the belltower. Other parts were added in the 18th century. Inside, the chancel has elaborate late Gothic vaulting; the ornate *retablo* is a fine 17th-century work; look out for the beautiful 14th-century baptismal font still in use.

The town has a **tourist office** ① *C Paseo del Moro 2, T954-883562, turismo@ cazalladelasierra.es, Tue-Wed 1000-1400, Thu 1000-1400, 1600-1800 (1800-2000 summer), Fri-Sat 1000-1400, 1600-1900 (1800-2100 summer), Sun 1100-1300*, with limited material on the area.

## Essential Around Sevilla city

### Getting around

It's easy to get out of Sevilla by bus to the main towns listed in the text, although travelling by car would give you more freedom. There are trains from Sevilla to Cazalla de la Sierra in the Sierra Morena but Cazalla train station is 7 km away from the town, so is not very convenient.

### When to go

The best time to visit is spring or autumn, because July and August are baking hot, although temperatures in the Sierra Morena are a bit cooler than elsewhere in Sevilla province due to the higher altitude.

### Time required

Allow at least a day in the Sierra Morena, a few days for towns east of Sevilla.

There are several marked **walking trails** in the Cazalla area. One of the best is Sendero Las Laderas, which begins from the bottom of the street that runs through the Plaza Mayor past the old town hall. It heads down to the river Huéznar and doubles back through woodland to the town; it takes 1½ hours, but you can extend the walk or even follow the river down to **El Pedroso**, a livestock town with a good hotel; see Where to stay, below. Visit the tourist office for maps.

### Constantina

This town, said to be named after the emperor Constantine, is a likeable village topped by a medieval castle with Moorish origins. In the narrow streets of the *morería* below are several fine mansions, while the parish church of Santa María de la Encarnación has a *mudéjar* tower and a Plateresque doorway. The town is the main centre for the Sierra del Norte natural park, which covers some 1650 sq km of the Sierra Morena. It's home to several species of raptor, as well as otters and wild boar. There's a visitor information centre, **El Robledo** ① *T955-889593, Wed-Sun 1000-1400, 1600-1800 (1700-2000 summer)*, on the western edge of town. The office has leaflets on the marked walking trails in the area and in autumn run guided walks that focus on the astonishing variety of wild mushrooms in the area.

## Listings Sierra Morena

### Where to stay

#### Cazalla de la Sierra

**€€ La Posada del Moro**
*Paseo del Moro s/n, T954-884858, www. laposadadelmoro.com.*
This excellent and welcoming hotel is in Cazalla itself and is remarkably good value. It's got much rural elegance, with the emphasis on comfort, and has a

pool, pretty garden, and a restaurant that will tempt you to prolong your stay. Recommended.

**€€ Las Navezuelas**
*Ctra Cazalla-El Robledo s/n, T954-884764, www.lasnavezuelas.com.*
Another charming rural establishment, set in a whitewashed *cortijo* with a restored olive mill and good pool. There

are 6 appealing rustic rooms and a variety of self-contained cottages. The price includes breakfast, and the owners can advise on walks in the area and arrange horse riding.

### Constantina

**€ Albergue Juvenil**
*Cuesta Blanca s/n, T955-035886, www. inturjoven.com.*
This official youth hostel has fine facilities and twin rooms with bathroom. Funding issues meant that this was temporarily closed at last research.

### Transport

**Cazalla de la Sierra**
Cercanía trains run 3 times daily from **Sevilla** (1 hr 35 mins) via **El Pedroso**, but the station is 7 km from town on the road to Constantina; taxis meet the train. There are also daily **buses** (1 hr 20 mins), which are more convenient.

**Constantina**
Several daily buses run from Constantina to **Sevilla** (1 hr).

## Carmona

*sun-baked, sleepy agricultural town*

★The small town of Carmona, encircled by formidable defensive walls, is an easy day trip from Sevilla, only 36 km east of the city, but couldn't have a more different feel. Outside the old town is one of Andalucía's most interesting archaeological sites, an excavated Roman cemetery. Carmona also offers a couple of excellent luxury hotels in the old town; see Where to stay, below, for details.

### Alcázar de Abajo
*Mon-Sat 1000-1800, Sun 1000-1500. €2, free Mon.*

On arrival in Carmona, you'll immediately be struck by the bulky complex of the lower *alcázar*, looming over the narrow entrance gate known as the Puerta de Sevilla. Fortified by successive conquering powers from the Phoenicians to the Castillians, the fortress preserves structures and foundations from all these periods. After an audiovisual presentation, you can wander around the building, which sometimes has temporary exhibitions in one of its halls. There's an informative brochure that helps you pick out the different building stages of the walls. From the top there are worthwhile views over the town and the fertile plains below. The **tourist office** ① *Mon-Sat 1000-1800, Sun 1000-1500, www. turismo.carmona.org*, is located in the Puerta de Sevilla. They can provide a town map and other information.

From here you should wander up through the whitewashed old town, peering into corners. Within this walled area are several churches; Santa María la Mayor preserves the former mosque's Patio de Naranjos and has a good 16th-century *retablo*, while San Pedro has an attractive *mudéjar* tower. Behind Santa María is a small archaeological and historical museum. The town centres on the shady Plaza de San Fernando; nearby the Ayuntamiento has a well-crafted Roman mosaic of

## Haciendas

Much of Sevilla province is taken up by huge farms that produce vast quantities of citrus fruit, olives, beef and fighting bulls. They are privately owned; this *latifundia* system derives from the days of the Christian Reconquest, when vast parcels of land won from the Moors in battle were distributed among the military leaders. These divisions are still in place and mean that in general local workers can't own their own land but must work as seasonal *jornaleros* on the *haciendas*. The system has contributed to large-scale social inequality in Andalucía and produced much rural unrest, not least in the years leading up to the Spanish Civil War.

The centrepiece of a *hacienda* is the farmhouse, or *cortijo*, which is usually a very grand affair, a complex of elegant whitewashed buildings that often includes a chapel. Many *haciendas* offer accommodation that is typically very luxurious. They are also popular venues for weddings and other celebrations.

For a full list, contact the Sevilla tourist office, see page 38. Some of the best are:

**El Esparragal**, T955-782702, www.elesparragal.com. Famous and fabulous hacienda in grassy grounds 23 km north of Sevilla in Gerena. Top restaurant and stylish fittings.

**Hacienda Benazuza**, T955-703344, www.elbullihotel.com. Fabulously luxurious and run by Ferran Adrià, the famous Catalan chef. In Sanlúcar La Mayor, 22 km west of Sevilla. Closed in winter.

**Hacienda San Rafael**, T955-227196, www.haciendadesanrafael.com. Run by same owners as the Corral del Rey in Sevilla. Lovely, with flowering plants, spacious rooms, and a great pool. South of Sevilla, halfway to Jerez. Recommended.

Medusa in its central courtyard. It's also worth seeking out Plaza de Abastos, an attractive hidden space dedicated to the morning food market.

### Roman Necropolis
*Tue-Sun 1000-1700. Free.*

Walking down the hill from the Puerta de Sevilla, you'll come to a long square, Paseo del Estatuto (where the bus from Sevilla stops). At the far end of this, take the middle of the three streets, which after 10 minutes will bring you to this very rewarding site. A series of interesting tombs have been excavated; belonging to wealthy citizens, they were dug into the rock and crowned with marble or stone structures (none of which survive). You get disinterestedly guided about but can make your way down into many of them, including the massive Tomb of Servilia, daughter of the local governor, where fragments of wall paintings are conserved. Information is in Spanish and English; try and see the small museum before visiting the site as it puts the material in context.

## Where to stay

**€€€€ Casa de Carmona**
*Plaza de Lasso 1, T954-143300, www.
casadecarmona.com.*
A restored *palacio* in the heart of
Carmona's old town, this is furnished
in period style and has comfortable
rooms, a restaurant and a pool, which is
a godsend in this sun-beaten town. It's
a little down in the dumps compared to
past glories but still doesn't disappoint.

**€€€€ Parador del Rey Don Pedro**
*C Los Alcázares s/n, T954-141010, www.
parador.es.*
The upper Alcázar, once used as a palace
by the charismatic Pedro I, has been
partially restored to house this, one of
southern Spain's finest paradores. There
are great views over the town and the
plains below. Recommended.

**€ Pensión Comercio**
*C Torre del Oro 56, T954-140018.*
Right next to the impressive Puerta
de Sevilla and tucked inside the walls,
this is a spruce option that's good
value for Carmona. It has rooms with
or without bath, as well as a/c (if you
thought Sevilla was hot, try Carmona).
There's also a decent cheap restaurant
and cordial management.

## Restaurants

The accommodation options
above all have restaurants that are
recommended. Other options centre
around Plaza San Fernando, where
there are several tapas bars. The tourist
office has a leaflet describing a tapas
crawl around the town.

**€€ Molino de la Romera**
*C Sor Angela de la Cruz 8, halfway
between San Pedro Church and
the Alcázar, T954-142000, www.
molinodelaromera.com.*
This restaurant is set in an old olive mill
and serves good local cuisine on its
terrace, which gives views over the plains
below. The wide menu includes cheese
platters, *revueltos*, and game dishes.

## Transport

Buses run hourly on the hour weekdays
and a little less often at weekends from
the Prado de San Sebastián station in
**Sevilla**, 50 mins. These drop you off
and leave from the Paseo del Estatuto,
just downhill from the Puerta de Sevilla.
From the pretty Alameda nearby,
there are a couple of daily buses to
**Ecija** and **Córdoba**.

## Ecija

*baroque churches and abundant palacios*

Halfway between Sevilla and Córdoba, this place shouldn't be missed by those
with a liking for Baroque architecture, although try to get there early, as the
town is famous for its fearsome summer heat. Once an important Roman olive oil
town named Astigi, it enjoyed great prosperity from the 16th to 18th centuries
as the vast *latifundias* claimed in the Reconquest began to pay dividends to
their inheritors, if not to the landless labourers that sweated to cultivate them.

This wealth is reflected the town's attractive *palacios*. Ecija is also notable for its 18th-century church towers, built after the 1755 Lisbon earthquake toppled the existing steeples.

Located in the centre of town is a **tourist office** ① *C Elvira 1, T955-902933, www. turismoecija.com, Mon-Sat 1000-1400, 1700-1900 Sun 1000-1400*, with plenty to offer; the website is also good.

The grandest of Ecija's palaces is the **Palacio de Peñaflor** ① *C Castelar s/n, listed for extensive renovation at time of writing*. The curved exterior is striking; it's known locally as the house of the long balcony, this feature being nearly 60 m long. The façade is decorated with frescoes, while inside is a fine staircase topped by a cupola with extravagantly decorative stucco work. The central patio has a marble fountain and a colourful dado of agate and different hues of marble.

Another stately residence near the Plaza de España is **Palacio de Benameji** ① *Jun-Sep Tue-Fri 1000-1430, Sat 1000-1400, 2000-2200, Sun 1000-1500; Oct-May Tue-Fri 1000-1330, 1630-1830, Sat 1000-1400, 1730-2000, Sun 1000-1500; free*, which has been converted into a beautiful museum displaying Roman finds, as well as some exhibits on local culture, particularly horse breeding.

The churches are too plentiful to list in detail here, but you'll come across nearly all of them by strolling in the area around Plaza de España. Most of the towers are cheerfully coloured in bright yellow and blue ceramic tiles.

## Listings Ecija

### Where to stay

Ecija's accommodation options are limited.

**€€ Hotel Platería**
*C Platería 1, T955-902754, www. hotelplateria.net.*
Tucked away down a side road, the hospitable **Platería** has well-furnished modern rooms set around a central atrium. There's also an excellent low-priced restaurant. An all-round bargain.

### Restaurants

**€€ Las Ninfas**
*C Cánovas del Castillo 4, T955-904592.*
This stylish restaurant occupying part of the same *palacio* as the museum is decorated with various objets d'art

and offers well-prepared local cuisine, including some excellent steaks.

### Festivals

**Sep** The town's **feria** takes place for 6 days in the 2nd week of the month. There's also a *cante jondo* **flamenco festival** night, which attracts excellent performers.

### Transport

**Bus**
There are 10 weekday buses (4-5 at weekends) to and from Prado San Sebastián station in **Sevilla** (1 hr 15 mins). There are also 4 daily buses that run to **Córdoba** and a few to **Carmona** and **Osuna**.

South of Ecija, this little-visited town is a ducal seat which owes most of its monuments to the wealthy Girón family, who held the title from the 16th century onwards. Osuna had been an important Iberian and then Roman town (Urso).

The town is situated on a steep hill; in the centre, in a characterful historic building that was once a brothel and theatre before being converted to the town grain store in the 18th century, stands the **tourist office** ⓘ *C Carrera 82, T954-815732, www.turismosuna.org, Tue-Sat 0930-1330, 1600-1800, Sun 0930-1330.*

The top of the hill is dominated by two buildings, the collegiate church and the old university. **Santa María de la Asunción** ⓘ *admission by guided tour Tue-Sun 1000-1330, 1530-1830 (1600-1900 summer), €2.50,* was founded in the mid-16th century by Juan Téllez Girón, who spared no expense in the construction. It's a beautifully proportioned Renaissance building (although there are later additions) in creamy stone. The Plateresque west portal looks out over the town and rolling plains. The interior is harmoniously arched and has a series of excellent paintings by Ribera, including a Crucifixion and a harried-looking San Jerónimo in the sacristy. The small cloister is another highlight, but the most exciting space is the pantheon of the Dukes of Osuna, an atmospheric and highly ornamented Plateresque crypt.

The university stands behind the church and has a fine patio with a pure Renaissance simplicity to it.

In the town below, there are several other churches worth visiting, including the Iglesia de la Merced, which has a barrel-vaulted ceiling.

## Listings Osuna

### Where to stay

**€€€ Palacio Marqués de la Gomera**
*C San Pedro 20, T954-812223, www. hotelpalaciodelmarques.es.*
Where else would you want to stay in Osuna other than a palace? This place fits the bill perfectly, set around a round-arched patio. The 18th-century building is furnished in period style. Rooms on the upper level are more attractive (and pricier) with wooden ceilings, but all are spacious and good value. The hotel also has 2 restaurants and a small garden.

### Transport

**Bus**
There are 6 daily buses to Osuna from **Sevilla**'s Prado de San Sebastián bus station. There are also buses to **Ecija**, **Antequera** and a couple on to **Málaga** itself.

# Background
## Andalucía

# History

Spain's proximity to Africa meant that Andalucía was one of Europe's frontlines for migrating hominids from the south. Discoveries near Burgos, in Spain's north attest that prehistoric humans inhabited the peninsula 1.3 million years ago; these are the oldest known hominid remains in Western Europe. Andalucía was a likely entry point.

Around the turn of the first millennium, the face of the region was changing significantly. The people named as **Iberians** in later texts, and probably of local origin, inhabited the area and were joined by some **Celts**, although these peoples predominantly settled in the north of the peninsula. The Iberians had two distinct languages, unrelated to the Indo-European family, and benefited significantly from the arrival of another group, the **Phoenicians**.

These master sailors and merchants from the Levant set up many trading stations on the Andalucían coast. The Phoenicians set about trading with the Iberians, and began extensive mining operations, extracting gold, silver and copper from Andalucía's richly endowed soils.

Profitable contact with this maritime superpower led to the emergence of the wealthy local **Tartessian** civilization. Famed in classical sources as a mystical region where demigods walked streets paved with gold, precious little is actually known about this culture. Although they developed writing, it is undeciphered. Although it seems that they had an efficiently controlled society, no site worthy of being identified as the capital, Tartessos, has been excavated. Seemingly based in the region around the Guadalquivir valley, including Carmona, the Tartessians were highly skilled craftsmen; the Carambolo hoard found in Sevilla province consists of astonishingly intricate and beautiful gold jewellery.

Towards the end of the sixth century BC, the Tartessian culture seems to disappear and Iberian settlements appear to have reverted to self-governing towns, usually fortified places on hilltops.

As Phoenician power waned, their heirs and descendants, the **Carthaginians**, increased their operations in the western Mediterranean and settled throughout Andalucía. While the Phoenicians had enjoyed a mostly prosperous and peaceful relationship with the local peoples, the Carthaginians were more concerned with conquest and, under **Hamilcar Barca** and his relatives **Hasdrubal** and **Hannibal**, they took control of much of southern Spain and increased mining operations. The Iberian tribes, who included the **Turdetanians**, the group that had inherited the Tartessian mantle in the Guadalquivir basin, seem to have had mixed relations with the Barcid rulers. Some towns accepted Carthaginian control, while others resisted it.

## Hispania

The Romans were bent on ending Punic power in the Mediterranean and soon realized that the peninsula was rapidly becoming a second Carthage. Roman troops arrived in Spain in 218 BC and Andalucía became one of the major theatres of the Second Punic War. Some of the local tribes, such as the Turdetanians, sided with the Romans against the Carthaginians and the final Roman victory came in 206 BC, at the Battle of Ilipa near Sevilla. The Carthaginians were kicked out of the peninsula.

During the war, the Romans had established the city of Itálica near Sevilla as a rest camp for dissatisfied Italian troops but it was only some time after the end of hostilities that the Romans appear to have developed an interest in the peninsula itself. Realizing the vast resources of the region, they set about conquering the whole of Hispania, a feat that they did not accomplish until late in the first century BC. It was the Romans that first created the idea of Spain as a single geographical entity, a concept it has struggled with ever since.

The wealth of Hispania meant that it became an important pawn in the power struggles of the Roman republic and it was in Andalucía, near modern Bailén, that **Julius Caesar** finally defeated Pompey's forces in 45 BC. With peace established, Caesar set about establishing colonies in earnest; many of Andalucía's towns and cities were built or rebuilt by the Romans in this period. Julius knew the region pretty well; he had campaigned here in 68 BC and later had been governor of Hispania Ulterior. The contacts he had made during this period served him well and Caesar rewarded the towns that had helped him against Pompey, such as Sevilla, by conferring full Roman citizenship on the inhabitants. Later, Vespasian granted these rights to the whole of the peninsula.

**Augustus** redivided Hispania into three provinces; the southernmost, **Baetica**, roughly corresponded to modern Andalucía. Initially administered from Córdoba, the capital was switched to Hispalis (Sevilla), which, along with neighbouring Itálica, prospered under the Imperial regime. The south of Spain became a real Roman heartland, the most Roman of the Roman colonies. Itálica was the birthplace of the Emperor Trajan and sometime home of his protegé Hadrian. The first century AD was a time of much peace and prosperity and Andalucía's grandest Roman remains date largely from this period.

It was probably during this century that the bustling Andalucían ports heard their first whisperings of Christianity, which arrived early in the peninsula. Around this time, too, a Jewish population began to build up; the beginnings of what was a crucial segment of Andalucían society for 1500 years.

A gradual decline began late in the second century AD, with raids from North Africa nibbling at the edges of a weakening empire. Christianity had become a dominant force, but religious squabblings exacerbated rather than eased the tension.

In the fifth century, as the Roman order tottered, various barbarian groups streamed across the Pyrenees and created havoc. **Alans** and **Vandals** established themselves in the south of Spain; it has been (almost certainly erroneously) suggested that the latter group lent their name to Andalucía. The Romans enlisted the Visigoths to restore order on their behalf. This they succeeded in doing, but they liked the look of the land and returned for good after they lost control of their French territories. After a period of much destruction and chaos, a fairly tenuous Visigothic control ensued. They used Sevilla as an early capital, but later transferred their seat of power to Toledo.

## BACKGROUND
## San Isidoro

*"No one can gain a full understanding of Spain without a knowledge of Saint Isidore" – Richard Ford*

Born in AD 560, Isidoro succeeded his brother Leandro as Bishop of Sevilla. One of the most important intellectual figures of the Middle Ages, his prolific writings cover all subjects and were still popular at the time of the Renaissance. His *Etymologiae* was one of the first secular books in print when it appeared in AD 1472. The first encyclopedia written in the Christian west, it became the primary source for the 154 classical authors that Isidoro quoted. He also wrote on music, law, history and jurisprudence as well as doctrinal matters.

Isidoro is also recognized as an important church reformer and was responsible for the production of the so-called Mozarabic rite which is still practised in Toledo Cathedral today. His writings were an attempt to restore vigour and direction to a church that was in decline following the Visigothic invasions.

Another important element to Isidoro's writings were his prophecies, based both on the Bible and classical references. This element of his writings appealed to later generations living in the shadow of the Muslim conquests and was to be the source of many stories and legends. Following the expulsion of the Moors it seemed to some that an ancient prophecy was about to be fulfilled.

Isidoro died in Sevilla in AD 636 and his writings continued to inspire Spain for the next nine centuries. His body is now in León, moved there by Fernando I of Castilla who repatriated it to the Christian north around AD 1060.

## The Visigoths

While there is little enough archaeological and historical evidence from this period, what has been found shows that the Visigoths had inherited Roman customs and architecture to a large degree, while many finds exhibit highly sophisticated carving and metalworking techniques. The bishop and writer San Isidoro produced some of Europe's most important post-Roman texts from his base in Sevilla; see box, above. There were likely comparatively few Visigoths; a small warrior class ruling with military strength best fits the evidence, and they seem to have fairly rapidly become absorbed into the local culture.

The seventh century saw numerous changes of rulers, many of whom imposed increasingly severe strictures on the substantial Jewish population of the peninsula. Restrictions on owning property, attempted forced conversions and other impositions foreshadowed much later events in Spain. The Visigoths possibly paid a heavy price for this persecution; several historians opine that the Moorish invasion was substantially aided by the support of Jewish communities that (rightly, as it turned out) viewed the conquerors as liberators.

## Al-Andalus

In AD 711 an event occurred that was to define Spanish history for the next eight centuries. The teachings of Mohammed had swept across North Africa and the Moors were to take most of Spain before the prophet had been dead for even a century. After a number of exploratory raids, Tarik, governor of Tanger, crossed the straits with a small force of mostly Berber soldiers. Joined by a larger force under the command of the governor of North Africa, Musa ibn-Nusair, the Moors then defeated and slew the Visigothic king Roderic somewhere near Tarifa. The conquests continued under Musa's son Abd al-Aziz until almost the whole peninsula was in Moorish hands; the conquest had taken less than three years, an extraordinary feat. Soon the Muslim armies were well advanced on the *autoroutes* of southern France.

The Moors named their Iberian dominions Al-Andalus and while these lands grew and shrunk over time, the heartland was always in the south. Romantic depictions of Al-Andalus as a multicultural paradise are way off the mark; the situation is best described by Richard Fletcher as one of "grudging toleration, but toleration nonetheless". Christians and Jews were allowed relative freedom of worship and examples of persecution are comparatively few. Moorish texts throughout the history of Al-Andalus reveal a condescending attitude towards non-Muslims (and vice-versa in Christian parts of Spain), but it is probable that in day-to-day life there was large-scale cultural contact, a process described by Spanish historians as *convivencia* (cohabitation). The conversion of Christians and Jews to Islam was a gradual but constant process; this was no doubt given additional impetus by the fact that Muslims didn't pay any tax beyond the alms required as part of their faith. Christian converts to Islam were known as *muwallads*, while those who remained Christian under the rule of the Moors are called *mozárabes* or Mozarabs.

Arabic rapidly became the major language of southern Spain, even among non-Muslims. The number of Arabic words in modern Spanish attests to this. Many of them refer to agriculture and crops; the Moors brought with them vastly improved farming and irrigation methods, as well as a host of fruits and vegetables not grown before on the peninsula's soil. This, combined with wide and profitable trading routes in the Mediterranean, meant that Al-Andalus began to thrive economically, which must have assisted in the pacification of the region. Córdoba's Mezquita, begun in the eighth century, was expanded and made richer in various phases through this period; this can be seen as reflecting both the growing wealth and the increasing number of worshippers.

## Christian kingdoms

Geography divides Spain into distinct regions, which have tended to persist through time, and it was one of these – Asturias – that the Moors had trouble with. They were defeated in what was presumably a minor skirmish in AD 717 at Covadonga, in the far northern mountains. It was hardly a crippling blow to the Moors, but it probably sowed the seeds of what became the **Asturian** and **Leonese** monarchy. They established an organized little kingdom of sorts with a capital that shifted about but settled on Oviedo in AD 808.

The Asturian kingdom began to grow in strength and the long process of the *Reconquista*, the Christian reconquest of the peninsula, began. As the Christians moved south, they re-settled many towns and villages that had lain in ruins since Roman times.

Both the Christian and Muslim powers were painfully aware of their vulnerability and constructed a series of massive fortresses that faced each other across the central plains. The Muslim fortresses were particularly formidable; high eyries with commanding positions, accurately named the 'front teeth' of Al-Andalus. Relations between Christian and Muslim Spain were curious. While there were frequent campaigns, raids and battles, there was also a high level of peaceful contact and diplomacy.

The caliphate faced a very real threat from the Fatimid dynasty in North Africa and campaigning in the Christian north was one way to fund the fortification of the Mediterranean coast. No-one campaigned more successfully than the formidable Al-Manzur, succeeding in sacking almost every city in Northern Spain in a 30-year campaign of terror. Al-Manzur was succeeded by his equally adept son Abd al-Malik, but when he died young in 1008, the caliphate disintegrated with two rival Ummayad claimants seeking to fill the power vacuum.

Twenty years of civil war followed. Both sides employed a variety of Christian and Muslim mercenaries to prosecute their claims to the caliphal throne; the situation was bloody and chaotic in the extreme. When the latest puppet caliph was deposed in 1031, any pretence of centralized government evaporated and Berber generals, regional administrators and local opportunists seized power in towns across Al-Andalus, forming the small city-states known as the *taifa* kingdoms; *taifa* means faction in Arabic.

This first *taifa* period lasted for most of the rest of the 11th century and in many ways sounded an early death-knell for Muslim Spain. Petty rivalries between the neighbouring *taifas* led to recruitment of Christian military aid in exchange for large sums of cash. This influx led in turn to the strengthening of the northern kingdoms and many *taifas* were then forced to pay tribute, or protection money, to Christian rulers or face obliteration.

The major *taifas* in Andalucía were Sevilla and Granada, which gradually swallowed up several of their smaller neighbours. The Abbadid rulers of Sevilla led a hedonistic life, the kings Al-Mu'tadid and his son Al-Mu'tamid penning poetry between revelries and romantic liaisons. A pogrom against the Jewish population in 1066 indicated that there was little urban contentment behind the luxuriant façade.

The Christian north lost little time in taking advantage of the weak *taifa* states. As well as exacting punitive tribute, the Castilian king Alfonso VI had his eye on conquests and crossed far beyond the former frontline of the Duero valley. His capture of highly symbolic Toledo, the old Visigothic capital and Christian centre, in 1085, finally set alarm bells ringing in the verse-addled brains of the *taifa* kings.

They realized they needed help, and they called for it across the Straits to Morocco. Since the middle of the 11th century, a group of tribesmen known as the **Almoravids** had been establishing control there and their leader, Yusuf, was invited across to Al-Andalus to help combat Alfonso VI. A more unlikely alliance is hard to imagine; the Almoravids were barely-literate desert warriors with a strong and fundamentalist Islamic faith, a complete contrast to the *taifa* rulers in their blossom-scented pleasure domes. The Almoravid armies defeated Alfonso near Badajoz in 1086 but were appalled at the state of Islam in Al-Andalus, so Yusuf decided to stay and establish a stricter observance. He rapidly destroyed the *taifa* system and established governors, answerable to Marrakech, in the major towns, including Sevilla, having whisked the poet-king off to wistful confinement in Fez.

Almoravid rule was marked by a more aggressive approach to the Christian north, which was matched by the other side. Any hope of retaking much territory soon subsided, as rebellions from the local Andalusi and pressure from another dynasty, the Almohads in Morocco, soon took their toll. This was compounded by another factor: tempted no doubt by big lunches, tapas, siestas and free-poured spirits, the hardline Almoravids were lapsing into softer ways. Control again dissolved into local *taifas*.

The Almohads, who by now controlled Morocco, began crossing the Straits to intervene in Andalusi military affairs. Although similarly named and equally hard line in their Islamism, the Almohads were significantly different to the Almoravids, with a canny grasp of politics and advanced military tactics. They gained control over the whole of what is now Andalucía by about 1172. Much surviving military architecture in Andalucía was built by the Almohads, including the great walls and towers of Sevilla. Yet they too lapsed into decadence, and bungled planning led to the very costly military defeat at Las Navas de Tolosa at the hands of Alfonso VIII in 1212. This was a major blow. Alfonso's son Fernando III (1217-1252) capitalized on his father's success, taking Córdoba in 1236, Jaén, the 'Iron Gate' of Andalucía, in 1246, and then Sevilla, the Almohad capital, in 1248, after a two-year siege. The loss of the most important city of Al-Andalus, mourned across the whole Muslim world, was effectively the end of Moorish power in Spain, although the emirate of Granada lingered on for another 250 years. Fernando, sainted for his efforts, kicked out all Sevilla's Moorish inhabitants, setting a pattern of intolerance towards the *mudéjares*, as those Muslims who lived under Christian rule came to be called.

What was left of Muslim Spain was the emirate of Granada. The nobleman Mohammed Ibn-Yusuf Ibn-Nasr set himself up here as ruler in 1237 and gave his name to the Nasrid dynasty. He sent a detachment of troops to help besiege Sevilla, a humiliation that eloquently shows how little real power he had.

Meanwhile, the Christians were consolidating their hold on most of Andalucía, building churches and cathedrals over the mosques they found and trying to find settlers to work the vast new lands at their disposal as many of the Moors had fled to the kingdom of Granada or across the sea to North Africa. Nobles involved in the *Reconquista* claimed vast tracts of territory; estates known as *latifundias* that still exist today and that have been the cause of numerous social problems in Andalucía over the centuries.

The Nasrid kingdom continued to survive, partly because its boundaries were extremely well fortified with a series of thousands of defensive towers. In the second half of the 14th century the enlightened Castilian king Pedro I was employing Moorish craftsmen to recreate Sevilla's Alcázar in sumptuous style.

## The Golden Age

In the 15th century, there were regular rebellions and much kinstrife over succession in the Nasrid kingdom, which was beginning to seem ripe for the plucking. One of the reasons this hadn't yet happened was that the Christian kingdoms were involved in similar succession disputes. Then, in 1469, an event occurred that was to spell the end for the Moorish kingdom and have a massive impact on the history of the world. The heir to the Aragonese throne, Fernando, married Isabel, heiress of Castilla, in a secret ceremony in Valladolid. The implications were enormous. Aragón was still a power in the Mediterranean (Fernando was also king of Sicily) and Castilla's domain covered much of the peninsula. The unification under the *Reyes Católicos*, as the monarchs became known, marked the beginnings of Spain as we know it today. Things didn't go smoothly at first, however. There were plenty of opponents to the union and forces in support of Juana, Isabel's elder (but claimed by her to be illegitimate) sister waged wars across Castilla.

When the north was once more at peace, the monarchs found that they ruled the entire peninsula except for Portugal, with which a peace had just been negotiated, the small mountain kingdom of Navarra, which Fernando stood a decent chance of inheriting at some stage anyway, and the decidedly un-Catholic Nasrids in their sumptuous southern palaces. The writing was on the wall and Fernando and Isabel began their campaign.

The Catholic Monarchs had put an end to Al-Andalus, which had endured in various forms for the best part of 800 years. They celebrated in true Christian style by kicking the Jews out of Spain. Andalucía's Jewish population had been hugely significant for a millennium and a half, heavily involved in commerce, shipping and literature throughout the peninsula. But hatred of them had begun to grow in the 14th century and there had been many pogroms, including an especially vicious one in 1391, which began in Sevilla and spread to most other cities in Christian Spain. Many converted during these years to escape the murderous atmosphere; they became known as *conversos*. The decision to expel those who hadn't converted was far more that of the pious Isabel than the pragmatic Fernando and has to be seen in the light of the paranoid Christianizing climate. The Jews were given four months to leave the kingdom and even the *conversos* soon found themselves under the iron hammer of the Inquisition.

In 1492 Cristóbal Colón (Christopher Columbus) had been petitioning the royal couple for ships and funds to mount an expedition to sail westwards to the Indies. Finally granted his request, he set off from Palos de la Frontera near Huelva and, after a deal of hardship, reached what he thought was his goal. In the wake of Columbus's discovery, the treaty of Tordesillas in 1494 partitioned the Atlantic between Spain and Portugal and led to the era of Spanish colonization of the Americas. In many ways, this was an extension of the *Reconquista* as young men hardened on the Castilian and Extremaduran *meseta* crossed the seas with zeal for conquest, riches and land. Andalucía was both enriched and crippled by this exodus: while the cities flourished on the New World booty and trade, the countryside was denuded of people to work the land. The biggest winner proved to be Sevilla, which was granted a monopoly over New World trade by the Catholic Monarchs in 1503. It grew rapidly and became one of Western Europe's foremost cities. In 1519 another notable endeavour began here. Ferdinand Magellan set sail from Triana, via Sanlúcar de Barrameda, in an attempt to circumnavigate the world. He didn't make it, dying halfway, but one of the expedition's ships did. Skippered by a Basque, Juan Sebastián Elkano, it arrived some three years later.

Isabel died in 1504, but refused to settle her Castilian throne on her husband, Fernando, to his understandable annoyance, as the two had succeeded in uniting virtually the whole of modern Spain under their joint rule. The inheritance passed to their mad daughter, Juana la Loca, and her husband, Felipe of Burgundy (el Hermoso or the Fair), who came to Spain in 1506 to claim their inheritance. Felipe soon died, however, and his wife's obvious inability to govern led to Fernando being recalled as regent of the united Spain until the couple's son, Carlos, came of age. During this period Fernando completed the boundaries of modern Spain by annexing Navarra. On his deathbed he reluctantly agreed to name Carlos heir to Aragón and its territories, thus preserving the unity he and Isabel had forged. Carlos I of Spain (Carlos V) inherited vast tracts of European land; Spain and southern Italy from his maternal grandparents, and Austria, Burgundy and the Low Countries from his paternal ones. He was shortly named Holy Roman Emperor and if all that worldly power weren't enough, his friend, aide and tutor, Adrian of Utrecht, was soon elected Pope.

The first two Habsburg monarchs, Carlos V and then his son Felipe II relied on the income from the colonies to pursue wars (often unwillingly) on several European fronts. It couldn't last; Spain's Golden Age has been likened by historian Felipe Fernández-Armesto to a dog walking on its hind legs. While Sevilla prospered from the American expansion, the provinces declined, hastened by a drain of citizens to the New World. The *comunero* revolt expressed the frustrations of a region that was once the focus of optimistic Christian conquest and agricultural wealth, but had now become peripheral to the designs of a 'foreign' monarchy. Resentment was exacerbated by the fact that the king still found it difficult to extract taxes from the *cortes* of Aragón or Catalunya, so Castilla (of which Andalucía was a part) bankrolled a disproportionate amount of the crippling costs of the running of a worldwide empire. The growing administrative requirements of managing an empire had forced the previously itinerant Castilian monarchs to choose a capital and Felipe II picked the small town of Madrid in 1561, something of a surprise, as Sevilla or Valladolid were more obvious choices. Although central, Madrid was remote, tucked away behind a shield of hills in the interior. This seemed in keeping with the somewhat paranoid nature of Habsburg rule. And beyond all other things, they were paranoid about threats to the Catholic religion; the biggest of which, of course, they perceived to be Protestantism. This paranoia was costly in the extreme.

# Decline of the empire

The struggle of the Spanish monarchy to control the spread of Protestantism was a major factor in the decline of the empire. Felipe II fought expensive and ultimately unwinnable wars in Flanders that bankrupted the state; while within the country the absolute ban on the works of heretical philosophers, scientists and theologists left Spain behind in Renaissance Europe. Felipe II's successors didn't have his strength of character; Felipe III was ineffectual and dominated by his advisors, while Felipe IV, so sensitively portrayed by Velázquez, tried hard but was indecisive and unfortunate. As well as being unwillingly involved in several costly wars overseas, there was also a major rebellion in Catalunya in the mid-17th century. The decline of the monarchy parallelled a physical decline in the monarchs, as the inbred Habsburgs became more and more deformed and weak; the last of them, Carlos II, was a tragic victim of contorted genetics who died childless and plunged the nation into a war of succession.

While the early 17th century saw the zenith of the Seville school of painting, the city was in decline; the expulsion of the *moriscos* had removed a vital labour force and merchants and bankers were packing up and going elsewhere as the crown's economic problems led to increasingly punitive taxation. The century saw several plagues in Andalucían cities and Sevilla lost an incredible half of its inhabitants in 1649.

The death of poor heirless Carlos II was a long time coming and foreign powers were circling to try and secure a favourable succession to the throne of Spain. Carlos eventually named the French duke Felipe de Bourbon as his successor, much to the concern of England and Holland, who declared war on France. War broke out throughout Spain until the conflict's eventual resolution at the Treaty of Utrecht; at which Britain received Gibraltar, and Spain also lost its Italian and Low Country possessions.

The Bourbon dynasty succeeded in bringing back a measure of stability and wealth to Spain in the 18th century. Sevilla's decline and the silting up of the Guadalquivir led to the monarchs establishing Cádiz as the centre for New World trade in its place and Spain's oldest city prospered again.

The 19th century in Andalucía and Spain was turbulent to say the least. The 18th century had ended with a Spanish-French conflict in the wake of the French revolution. Peace was made after two years, but worse was to follow. First was a heavy defeat for a joint Spanish-French navy by Nelson off Cabo Trafalgar near Cádiz. Next Napoleon tricked Carlos IV. Partitioning Portugal between France and Spain seemed like a good idea to Spain, which had always coveted its western neighbour. It wasn't until the French armies seemed more interested in Madrid than Lisbon that Carlos IV got the message. Forced to abdicate in favour of his rebellious son Fernando, he was then summoned to a conference with Bonaparte at Bayonne, with his son, wife and Manuel Godoy, his able and trusted adviser (who is often said to have been loved even more by the queen than the king). Napoleon had his own brother Joseph (known among Spaniards as *Pepe Botellas* for his heavy drinking) installed on the throne.

On 2 May 1808 (still a red-letter day in Spain), the people revolted against this arrogant gesture and Napoleon sent in the troops later that year. Soon after, a hastily assembled Spanish army inflicted a stunning defeat on the French at Bailén, near Jaén; the Spaniards were then joined by British and Portuguese forces and the ensuing few years are known in Spain as the Guerra de Independencia (War of Independence). The allied forces under Wellington won important battles after the initiative had been taken by the French. The behaviour of both sides was brutal both on and off the battlefield. Marshal Soult's long retreat across the region saw him loot town after town; his men robbed tombs and burned priceless archives. The allied forces were little better; the men Wellington had referred to as the 'scum of the earth' sacked the towns they conquered with similar destructiveness.

Significant numbers of Spaniards had been in favour of the French invasion and were opposed to the liberal republican movements that sprang up in its wake. In 1812, a revolutionary council in Cádiz, on the point of falling to the French, drafted a constitution proclaiming a democratic parliamentary monarchy of sorts. Liberals had high hopes that this would be brought into effect at the end of the war, but the returning king, Fernando, revoked it. Meanwhile, Spain was on the point of losing its South American colonies, which were being mobilized under *libertadores* such as Simón Bolívar. Spain sent troops to restore control; a thankless assignment for the soldiers involved. One of the armies was preparing to leave Cádiz in 1820 when the commander, Rafael de Riego, invoked the 1812 constitution and refused to fight under the 'unconstitutional' monarchy. Much of the army joined him and the king was forced to recognize the legality of the constitution. Things soon dissolved though, with the 'liberals' (the first use of the word) being split into factions and opposed by the church and aristocracy. Eventually, king Fernando called on the king of France to send an invading army; the liberals were driven backwards to Sevilla, then to Cádiz, where they were defeated and Riego taken to his execution in Madrid. In many ways this conflict mirrored the later Spanish Civil War. Riego, who remained (and remains) a hero of the democratically minded, did not die in vain; his stand impelled much of Europe on the road to constitutional democracy, although it took Spain itself over a century and a half to find democratic stability.

The remainder of the century was to see clash after clash of liberals against conservatives, progressive cities against reactionary countryside, restrictive centre against outward-looking periphery. Spain finally lost its empire, as the strife-torn homeland could do little against the independence movements of Latin America. When Fernando died, another war of succession broke out, this time between supporters of his brother Don Carlos and his infant daughter Isabella. The so-called Carlist Wars of 1833-1839, 1847-1849 (although this is sometimes not counted as one) and 1872-1876 were politically complex. Don Carlos represented conservatism and his support was drawn from a number of sources. Wealthy landowners, the church and the reactionary peasantry, with significant French support, lined up against the loyalist army, the liberals and the urban middle and working classes. In between and during the wars, a series of *pronunciamientos* (coups d'état) plagued the monarchy. In 1834, after Fernando's death, another, far less liberal constitution was drawn up. An important development for Andalucía took place in 1835 when the Prime Minister, desperate for funds to prosecute the war against the Carlists, confiscated church and monastery property in the Disentailment Act. The resulting sale of the vast estates aided nobody but the large landowners, who bought them up at bargain prices, further skewing the distribution of arable land in Andalucía towards the wealthy.

Despite the grinding poverty, the middle years of the 19th century saw the beginnings of what was eventually to save Andalucía: tourism. Travellers, such as Washington Irving, Richard Ford and Prosper Merimée, came to the region and enthralled the world with tales of sighing Moorish princesses, feisty *sevillanas*, bullfights, gypsies, bandits and passion. While to the 21st-century eye, the uncritical romanticism of these accounts is evident, they captured much of the magic that contemporary visitors still find in the region and have inspired generations of travellers to investigate Spain's south.

During the third Carlist war, the king abdicated and the short-lived First Spanish Republic was proclaimed, ended by a military-led restoration a year later. The Carlists were defeated but remained strong and played a prominent part in the Spanish Civil War. (Indeed, there's still a Carlist party.) As if generations of war weren't enough, the wine industry of Andalucía received a crippling blow with the arrival of the phylloxera pest, which devastated the region.

The 1876 constitution proclaimed by the restored monarchy after the third Carlist war provided for a peaceful alternation of power between liberal and conservative parties. In the wake of decades of strikes and *pronunciamientos* this was not a bad solution and the introduction of the vote for the whole male population in 1892 offered much hope. The ongoing curse, however, was *caciquismo*, a system whereby elections and governments were hopelessly rigged by influential local groups of 'mates'.

Spain lost its last overseas possessions; Cuba, Puerto Rico and the Phillippines, in the 'Disaster' of 1898. The introspective turmoil caused by this event gave the name to the '1898 generation', a forward-thinking movement of artists, philosophers and poets among whom were numbered the poets Antonio Machado and Juan Ramón Jiménez, the philosophers José Ortega y Gasset and Miguel de Unamuno and the painter Ignacio de Zuloaga. It was a time of discontent, with regular strikes culminating in the Semana Trágica (tragic week) in Barcelona in 1909, a week of church-burning and rioting sparked by the government's decision to send a regiment of Catalan conscripts to fight in the 'dirty war' in Morocco; the revolt was then brutally suppressed by the army. The growing disaffection of farmworkers in Andalucía, forced for centuries into seasonal labour on the vast *latifundias* with no security and minimal earnings, led to a strong anarchist movement in the region. The CNT, the most prominent of the 20th-century anarchist confederations, was founded in Sevilla in 1910.

## The Second Republic

The early years of the 20th century saw repeated changes of government under King Alfonso XIII. A massive defeat in Morocco in 1921 increased the discontent with the monarch, but General Miguel Primo de Rivera, a native of Jerez de la Frontera, led a coup and installed himself as dictator under Alfonso in 1923. One of his projects was the grandiose Ibero-American exhibition in Sevilla. The preparation for this lavish event effectively created the modern city we know today and, despite bankrupting the city, set the framework for a 20th-century urban centre.

Primo de Rivera's rule was relatively benign, but growing discontent eventually forced the king to dismiss him. Having broken his coronation oath to uphold the constitution, Alfonso himself was soon toppled as republicanism swept the country. The anti-royalists achieved excellent results in elections in 1931 and the king drove to Cartagena and took a boat out of the country to exile. The Second Republic was joyfully proclaimed by the left.

Things moved quickly in the short period of the republic. The new leftist government moved fast to drastically reduce the church's power. The haste was ill-advised and triumphalist and served to severely antagonize the conservatives and the military. The granting of home rule to Catalunya was even more of a blow to the establishment and their belief in Spain as an indissoluble *patria*, or fatherland.

Through this period, there was increasing anarchist activity in Andalucía, where land was seized as a reaction to the archaic *latifundia* system under which prospects for the workers, who were virtually serfs, were nil. Anarchist cooperatives were formed to share labour and produce in many of the region's rural areas. Squabbling among leftist factions contributed to the government's lack of control of the country, which propelled the right to substantial gains in elections in 1933. Government was eventually formed by a centrist coalition, with the right powerful enough to heavily influence lawmaking. The 1933 elections also saw José Antonio Primo de Rivera, son of the old dictator, elected to a seat on a fascist platform. Although an idealist and no man of violence, he founded the Falange, a group of fascist youth that became an increasingly powerful force and one which was responsible for some of the most brutal deeds before, during and immediately after the Spanish Civil War.

The new government set about reversing the reforms of its predecessors; provocative and illegal infractions of labour laws by employers didn't help the workers' moods. Independence rumblings in Catalunya and the Basque country began to gather momentum, but it was in Asturias that the major confrontation took place. The left, mainly consisting of armed miners, seized the civil buildings of the province and the government response was harsh, with generals Goded and Franco embarking on a brutal spree of retribution with their well-trained Moroccan troops.

The left was outraged and the right feared complete revolution; the centre ceased to exist, as citizens and politicians were forced to one side or the other. The elections of February 1936 were very close, but the left unexpectedly defeated the right. In an increasingly violent climate, mobilized Socialist youth and the Falange were clashing daily, while land seizures continued. A group of generals began to plan a coup and in July 1936 a military conspiracy saw garrisons throughout Spain rise against the government and try to seize control of their provinces and towns. Within a few days, battle lines were clearly drawn between the Republicans (government) and the Nationalists, a coalition of military, Carlists, fascists and the Christian right. Most of northern Spain rapidly went under Nationalist control, while Madrid remained Republican. In Andalucía, Córdoba, Cádiz, Sevilla, Huelva and Granada were taken by Nationalists, but the remainder was in loyalist hands.

In the immediate aftermath of the uprising, frightening numbers of civilians were shot behind the lines, including the Granadan poet, Federico García Lorca. This brutality continued throughout the war, with chilling atrocities committed on both sides.

The most crucial blow of the war was struck early. Francisco Franco, one of the army's best generals, had been posted to the Canary Islands by the government, who were rightly fearful of coup attempts. As the uprising occurred, Franco was flown to Morocco where he took command of the crack North African legions. The difficulty was crossing into Spain: this was achieved in August in an airlift across the Straits of Gibraltar by German planes. Franco swiftly advanced through Andalucía where his battle-hardened troops met with little resistance. Meanwhile, the other main battle lines were north of Madrid and in Aragón, where the Republicans made a determined early push for Zaragoza.

At a meeting of the revolutionary generals in October 1936, Franco had himself declared *generalísimo*, the supreme commander of the Nationalists. Few could have suspected that he would rule the nation for nearly four decades. Although he had conquered swathes of Andalucía and Extremadura with little difficulty, the war wasn't to be as short as it might have appeared. Advancing on Madrid, he detoured to relieve the besieged garrison at Toledo; by the time he turned his attention back to the capital, the defences had been shored up and Madrid resisted throughout the war.

A key aspect of the Spanish Civil War was international involvement. Fascist Germany and Italy had troops to test, and a range of weaponry to play with; these countries gave massive aid to the Nationalist cause as a rehearsal for the Second World War, which was appearing increasingly inevitable. Russia provided the Republicans with some material, but inscrutable Stalin never committed his full support. Other countries, such as Britain, USA and France, disgracefully maintained a charade of international non-intervention despite the flagrant breaches by the above nations. Notwithstanding, thousands of volunteers mobilized to form the international brigades to help out the Republicans. Enlisting for idealistic reasons to combat the rise of fascism, many of these soldiers were writers and poets such as George Orwell and WH Auden.

Although Republican territory was split geographically, far more damage was done to their cause by ongoing and bitter infighting between anarchists, socialists, Soviet-backed communists and independent communists. There was constant struggling for power, political manoeuvring, backstabbing and outright violence, which the well-organized Nationalists must have watched with glee. The climax came in Barcelona in May 1937, when the Communist party took up arms against the anarchists and the POUM, an independent communist group. The city declined into a mini civil war of its own until order was restored. Morale, however, had taken a fatal blow.

Cities continued to fall to the Nationalists, for whom the German Condor legion proved a decisive force. In the south, the armies were under the command of Gonzalo Queipo de Llano, who though of broadly republican sympathies, was one of the original conspirators, and had expertly taken Sevilla at the beginning of things. Although his propaganda broadcasts throughout the war revealed him to be a kind of psychopathic humourist, this charismatic aristocrat was an impressive general and took Málaga in early 1937. Fleeing refugees were massacred by tanks and aircraft. Republican hopes now rested solely in the outbreak of a Europe-wide war. Franco had set up base appropriately in deeply conservative Burgos; Nationalist territory was the venue for many brutal reprisals against civilians perceived as leftist, unionist, democratic, or owning a tasty little piece of land on the edge of the village. Republican atrocities in many areas were equally appalling although rarely sanctioned or perpetrated by the government.

The Republicans made a couple of last-ditch efforts in early 1938 at Teruel and in the Ebro valley but were beaten in some of the most gruelling fighting of the Civil War. The Nationalists reached the Mediterranean, dividing Catalunya from the rest of Republican territory and, after the ill-fated Republican offensive over the Ebro, putting Barcelona under intense pressure; it finally fell in January 1939. Even at this late stage, given united resistance, the Republicans could have held out a while longer and the World War might have prevented a Franco victory, but it wasn't to be. The fighting spirit had largely dissipated and the infighting led to meek capitulation. Franco entered Madrid and the war was declared over on 1 April 1939.

If Republicans were hoping that this would signal the end of the slaughter and bloodshed, they didn't know the *generalísimo* well enough. A vengeful spate of executions, lynchings, imprisonments and torture ensued and the dull weight of the new regime stifled growth and optimism. Although many thousands of Spaniards fought in the Second World War (on both sides), Spain remained nominally neutral. After meeting Franco at Hendaye, Hitler declared that he would prefer to have three or four teeth removed than have to do so again. Franco had his eye on French Morocco and was hoping to be granted it for minimal Spanish involvement; Hitler accurately realized that the country had little more to give in the way of war effort and didn't offer an alliance.

The post-war years were tough in Spain, particularly in poverty-stricken Andalucía, where the old system was back in place and the workers penniless. Franco was an international outcast and the 1940s and 1950s were bleak times. Thousands of Andalucíans left in search of employment and a better life in Europe, the USA and Latin America. The Cold War was to prove Spain's saviour. Franco was nothing if not anti-communist and the USA began to see his potential as an ally. Eisenhower offered to provide a massive aid package in exchange for Spanish support against the Eastern Bloc. In practice, this meant the creation of American airbases on Spanish soil; one of the biggest is at Rota, just outside Cádiz.

The dollars were dirty, but the country made the most of them; Spain boomed in the 1960s as industry finally took off and the flood of tourism to the Andalucían coasts began in earnest. But dictatorship was no longer fashionable in western Europe and Spain was regarded as a slightly embarassing cousin. It was not invited to join the European Economic Community (EEC) and it seemed as if nothing was going to really change until Franco died. He finally did, in 1975, and his appointed successor, King Juan Carlos I, the grandson of Alfonso XIII, took the throne of a country burning with democratic desires.

## La Transición

The king was initially predicted to be just a pet of Franco's and therefore committed to maintaining the stultifying status quo, but he surprised everyone by acting swiftly to appoint the young Adolfo Suárez as prime minister. Suárez bullied the parliament into approving a new parliamentary system; political parties were legalized in 1977 and elections held in June that year. The return to democracy was known as *la transición*; the accompanying cultural explosion became known as *la movida (madrileña)*. Suárez's centrist party triumphed and he continued his reforms. The 1978 constitution declared Spain a parliamentary monarchy with no official religion; Franco must have turned in his grave and Suárez faced increasing opposition from the conservative elements in his own party. He resigned in 1981 and as his successor was preparing to take power, the good old Spanish tradition of the *pronunciamiento* came to the fore once again. A detachment of *Guardia Civil* stormed parliament in their comedy hats and Lieutenant Colonel Tejero, pistol waving and moustache twitching, demanded everyone hit the floor. After a tense few hours in which it seemed that the army might come out in support of Tejero, the king remained calm and, dressed in his capacity as head of the armed forces, assured the people of his commitment to democracy. The coup attempt thus failed and Juan Carlos was seen in an even better light.

In 1982, the Socialist government (PSOE) of Felipe González was elected. Hailing from Sevilla, he was committed to improving conditions and infrastructure in his native Andalucía. The single most important legislation since the return to democracy was the creation of the *comunidades autónomas*, in which the regions of Spain were given their own parliaments, which operate with varying degrees of freedom from the central government. This came to bear in 1983, although it was a process initiated by Suárez. Sevilla became the capital of the Andalucían region.

The Socialists held power for 14 years and oversaw Spain's entry into the EEC (now EU) in 1986, from which it has benefited immeasurably, although rural Andalucía remains poor by western European standards. But mutterings of several scandals began to plague the PSOE government and González was really disgraced when he was implicated in having commissioned death squads with the aim of terrorizing the Basques into renouncing terrorism, which few of them supported in any case.

# Culture

## Architecture

Spain's architectural heritage is one of Europe's richest and certainly its most diverse, due in large part to the dual influences of European Christian and Islamic styles during the eight centuries of Moorish presence in the peninsula. Another factor is economic: both during the *Reconquista* and in the wake of the discovery of the Americas, money seemed limitless and vast building projects were undertaken. Entire treasure fleets were spent in erecting lavish churches and monasteries on previously Muslim soil, while the relationships with Islamic civilization spawned some fascinating styles unique to Spain. The Moors adorned their towns with sensuous palaces and elegant mosques, as well as employing compact climate-driven urban planning that still forms the hearts of most towns. In modern times Spain has shaken off the ponderous monumentalism of the Franco era and become something of a powerhouse of modern architecture.

The story of Spanish architecture really begins with the Romans, who colonized the peninsula and imposed their culture on it to a significant degree. More significant still is the legacy they left; architectural principles that endured and to some extent formed the basis for later peninsular styles.

There's not a wealth of outstanding monuments; **Itálica**, just outside Sevilla, is an impressive, if not especially well-preserved, Roman town. In many towns and villages you can see Roman fortifications and foundations under existing structures.

The first distinct period of Moorish architecture in Spain is that of the Umayyads who ruled as emirs, then as caliphs, from Córdoba from the eighth to 11th centuries. The period of the caliphate was the high point of Al-Andalus and some suitably sumptuous architecture remains.

The Almoravids contributed little to Andalucían architecture, but the Almohads brought their own architectural modifications with them. Based in Sevilla, their styles were not as flamboyant and relied heavily on ornamental brickwork. The supreme example of the period is the **Giralda tower** that once belonged to the Mosque in Sevilla and now forms part of the cathedral. The use of intricate wood-panelled ceilings began to be popular and the characteristic Andalucían azulejo decorative tiles were first used at this time. Over this period the horseshoe arch developed a point. The Almohads were great military architects and built or improved a large number of walls, fortresses and towers; these often have characteristic pointed battlements. The **Torre del Oro** in Sevilla is one of the most famous and attractive examples.

The climax of Moorish architecture ironically came when Al-Andalus was already doomed and had been reduced to the emirate of Granada. The Alcázar in Sevilla is a good example of the period, though actually constructed in Christian Spain; it is very Nasrid in character and Granadan craftsmen certainly worked on it.

As the Christians gradually took back Andalucía, they introduced their own styles, developed in the north with substantial influence from France and Italy. The Romanesque barely features in Andalucía; it was the Gothic style that influenced post-Reconquista church building in the 13th, 14th and 15th centuries. It was combined with styles learned under the Moors to form an Andalucían fusion known as Gothic-*mudéjar*. Many of the region's churches are constructed on these lines, typically featuring a rectangular floor plan with a triple nave surrounded by pillars, a polygonal chancel and square chapels. Gothic exterior buttresses were used and many had a bell tower decorated with ornate brickwork reminiscent of the Giralda, which was also rebuilt during this period.

The Andalucían Gothic style differs from the rest of the peninsula in its basic principles. Whereas in the north, the 'more space, less stone, more light' philosophy pervaded, practical considerations demanded different solutions in the south. One of these was space; the cathedrals normally occupied the site of the former mosque, which had square ground plans and were hemmed in by other buildings. Another was defence – churches and cathedrals had to be ready to double as fortresses in case of attack, so sturdy walls were of more importance than stained glass. Many of Andalucía's churches, built in the Gothic style, were heavily modified in succeeding centuries and present a blend of different architectures.

*Mudéjar* architecture spread quickly across Spain. Moorish architects and those who worked with them began to meld their Islamic tradition with the northern influences. The result is distinctive and pleasing, typified by the decorative use of brick and coloured tiles, with tall elegant bell towers a particular highlight. Another common feature is the highly elaborate wooden panelled ceilings, some of which are masterpieces. The word *artesonado* describes the most characteristic type of these. The style became popular nationwide; in certain areas, *mudéjar* remained a constant feature for over 500 years of building.

The final phase of Spanish Gothic was the Isabelline, or Flamboyant. Produced during and immediately after the reign of the Catholic Monarchs (hence the name), it borrowed decorative motifs from Islamic architecture to create an exuberant form characterized by highly elaborate façades carved with tendrils, sweeping curves and geometrical patterns.

The 16th century was a high point in Spanish power and wealth, when it expanded across the Atlantic, tapping riches that must have seemed limitless. Spanish Renaissance architecture reflected this, leading from the late Gothic style into the elaborate peninsular style known as Plateresque. Although the style originally relied heavily on Italian models, it soon took on specifically Spanish features. The word refers particularly to the façades of civil and religious buildings, characterized by decoration of shields and other heraldic motifs, as well as geometric and naturalistic patterns such as shells. The term comes from the word for silversmith, *platero*, as the level of intricacy of the stonework approached that of jewellery. Arches went back to the rounded and columns and piers became a riot of foliage and 'grotesque' scenes.

A classical revival put an end to much of the elaboration, as Renaissance architects concentrated on purity. To classical Greek features such as fluted columns and pediments were added large Italianate cupolas and domes. Spanish architects were apprenticed to Italian masters and returned to Spain with their ideas. Elegant interior patios in *palacios* are an especially attractive feature of the style, to be found across the country. Andalucía is a particularly rich storehouse of this style, where the master Diego de Siloé designed numerous cathedrals and churches. Fine 16th-century *palacios* can be found in nearly every town and city of Andalucía; often built in honey-coloured sandstone, these noble buildings were the homes of the aristocrats who had reaped the riches of the Reconquista and the new trade routes to the Americas.

The pure lines of this Renaissance classicism were soon to be transformed into a new style, Spanish Baroque. Although it started fairly soberly, it soon became rather ornamental, often being used to add elements to existing buildings. The Baroque was a time of great genius in architecture as in the other arts in Spain, as masters playfully explored the reaches of their imaginations; a strong reaction against the sober preceding style. Churches became ever larger, in part to justify the huge façades, and nobles indulged in one-upmanship, building ever-grander *palacios*. The façades themselves are typified by such features as pilasters (narrow piers descending to a point) and niches to hold statues. Andalucía has a vast array of Baroque churches; Sevilla in particular bristles with them. Smaller towns, such as Ecija, are also well endowed, as they both enjoyed significant agriculture-based prosperity during the period.

The Baroque became more ornate as time went on, reaching the extremes of Churrigueresque, named for the Churriguera brothers who worked in the late 17th and early 18th centuries. The result can be overelaborate but on occasion transcendentally beautiful. Vine tendrils and cherubs decorate façades and *retablos*, which seem intent on breaking every classical norm, twisting here, upside-down there and at their best seeming to capture motion.

Neoclassicism, encouraged by a new interest in the ancient civilizations of Greece and Rome, was an inevitable reaction to such *joie de vivre*. It again resorted to the cleaner lines of antiquity, which were used this time for public spaces as well as civic and religious buildings. Many plazas and town halls in Spain are in this style, which tended to flourish in the cities that were thriving in the late 18th and 19th centuries. The best examples use symmetry to achieve beauty and elegance, such as Sevilla's tobacco factory, which bridges Baroque and neoclassical styles.

Awakened interest in the days of Al-Andalus led to the neo-Moorish (or neo-*mudéjar*) style being used for public buildings and private residences. The most evident example of this is the fine ensemble of buildings constructed in Sevilla for the 1929 Ibero-American exhibition. Budgets were thrown out the window and the lavish pavilions are sumptuously decorated.

Elegance and whimsy never seemed to play much part in fascist architecture and during the Franco era Andalucía was subjected to an appalling series of ponderous concrete monoliths, all in the name of progress. A few avant-garde buildings managed to escape the drudgery from the 1950s on, but it was the dictator's death in 1975, followed by EEC membership in 1986, that really provided the impetus for change.

Andalucía is not at the forefront of Spain's modern architectural movements, but the World Expo in Sevilla in 1992 brought some of the big names in. Among the various innovative pavilions, Santiago Calatrava's sublime bridges stand out. The impressive Teatro de la Maestranza and public library also date from this period, while the newer Olympic stadium is a more recent offering. Sevilla's fantastic Parasol building, daringly built over a square in the old town, is the latest spectacular construction. Elsewhere, the focus has been on softening the harsh Francoist lines of the cities' 20th-century expansions. In most places this has been quietly successful.

## Art

In the first millennium BC, Iberian cultures produced fine jewellery from gold and silver, as well as some remarkable sculpture and ceramics.These influences derived from contact with trading posts set up by the Phoenicians, who also left artistic evidence of their presence, mostly in the port cities they established. Similarly, the Romans brought their own artistic styles to the peninsula and there are many cultural remnants, including some fine sculpture and a number of elaborate mosaic floors. Later, the Visigoths were skilled artists and craftspeople and produced many fine pieces, most notably in metalwork.

The majority of the artistic heritage left by the Moors is tied up in their architecture (see below). As Islamic tradition has tended to veer away from the portrayal of human or animal figures, the norm was intricate applied decoration with calligraphic, geometric and vegetal themes predominating. Superb panelled ceilings are a feature of Almohad architecture; a particularly attractive style being that known as *artesonado*, in which the concave panels are bordered with elaborate inlay work. During this period, glazed tiles known as azulejos began to be produced; these continue to be a feature of Andalucían craftsmanship.

The gradual process of the *Reconquista* brought Christian styles into Andalucía. Generally speaking, the Gothic, which had arrived in Spain both overland from France and across the Mediterranean from Italy, was the first post-Moorish style in Andalucía. Over time, Gothic sculpture achieved greater naturalism and became more ornate, culminating in the technical mastery of sculptors and painters, such as Pedro Millán, Pieter Dancart (who is responsible for the massive altarpiece of Sevilla's cathedral) and Alejo Fernández, all of whom were from or heavily influenced by northern Europe.

Though to begin with, the finest artists were working in Northern Spain, Andalucía soon could boast several notable figures of its own. In the wake of the Christian conquest of Granada, the Catholic Monarchs and their successor Carlos V went on a building spree. The Spanish Renaissance drew heavily on the Italian but developed its own style. Perhaps the finest 16th-century figure is Pedro de Campaña, a Fleming whose exalted talent went largely unrecognized in his own time. His altarpiece of the Purification of Mary in Sevilla's cathedral is particularly outstanding.

As the Renaissance progressed, naturalism in painting increased, leading into the Golden Age of Spanish art. As Sevilla prospered on New World riches, the city became a centre for artists, who found wealthy patrons in abundance. Pre-eminent among all was Diego Rodríguez de Silva Velázquez (1599-1660), who started his career there before moving to Madrid to become a court painter. Another remarkable painter working in Sevilla was Francisco de Zurbarán (1598-1664) whose idiosyncratic style often focuses on superbly rendered white garments in a dark, brooding background, a metaphor for the subjects themselves, who were frequently priests. During Zurbarán's later years, he was eclipsed in the Sevilla popularity stakes by Bartolomé Esteban Murillo (1618-1682). While at first glance his paintings can seem heavy on the sentimentality, they tend to focus on the space between the central characters, who interact with glances or gestures of great power and meaning. Juan Valdés Leal painted many churches and monasteries in Sevilla; his greatest works are the macabre realist paintings in the Hospital de la Caridad. The sombre tone struck by these works reflects the decline of the once-great mercantile city.

At this time, the sculptor Juan Martínez Montañés carved numerous figures, *retablos* and *pasos* (ornamental floats for religious processions) in wood. Pedro Roldán, Juan de Mesa and Pedro de Mena were other important Baroque sculptors from this period, as was Alonso Cano, a crotchety but talented painter and sculptor working from Granada. The main focus of this medium continued to be ecclesiastic; *retablos* became ever larger and more ornate, commissioned by nobles to gain favour with the church and improve their chances in the afterlife.

The 18th and early 19th centuries saw fairly characterless art produced under the new dynasty of Bourbon kings. Tapestry production increased markedly but never scaled the heights of the earlier Flemish masterpieces. One man who produced pictures for tapestries was the master of 19th-century art, Francisco Goya. Goya was a remarkable figure whose finest works included both paintings and etchings; there's a handful of his work scattered around Andalucía's galleries, but the best examples are in Madrid's Prado and in the north.

After Goya, the 19th century produced few works of note as Spain tore itself apart in a series of brutal wars and conflicts. Perhaps in reaction to this, the *costumbrista* tradition developed; these painters and writers focused on portraying Spanish life; their depictions often revolving around nostalgia and stereotypes. Among the best were the Bécquer family: José; his cousin Joaquín; and his son Valeriano, whose brother Gustavo Adolfo was one of the period's best-known poets.

The Civil War was to have a serious effect on art in Spain, as a majority of artists sided with the Republic and fled Spain with their defeat. Franco was far from an enlightened patron of the arts and his occupancy was a monotonous time. Times have changed, however, and the regional governments, including the Andalucían, are extremely supportive of local artists these days and the museums in each provincial capital usually have a good collection of modern works.

# BACKGROUND

## Antonio Machado

*Mi infancia son recuerdos de un patio de Sevilla, / y un huerto claro donde madura el limonero; / mi juventud, veinte años en tierras de Castilla; / mi historia, algunos casos que recordar no quiero*

*My childhood is memories of a patio in Sevilla, / and of a light-filled garden where the lemon tree grows / My youth, twenty years in the lands of Castilla / My story, some happenings I wish not to remember*

Along with Federico García Lorca, Antonio Machado was Spain's greatest 20th-century poet. Part of the so-called Generation of '98 who struggled to re-evaluate Spain in the wake of losing its last colonial possessions in 1898, he was born in 1875 in Sevilla.

Growing up mostly in Madrid, he spent time in France and then lived and worked in Soria, in Castilla; much of his poetry is redolent of the harsh landscapes of that region. His solitude was exacerbated when his young wife Leonor died after three years of marriage. He then moved to Baeza, where he taught French in a local school. Like the poetry written in Soria, his work in Andalucía reflected his profound feelings for the landscape.

Machado was a staunch defender of the Republic and became something of a bard of the Civil War. Forced to flee with thousands of refugees as the Republic fell, he died not long after, in 1939, in a pensión in southern France. His will to live was dealt a bitter blow by the triumph of fascism, while his health had suffered badly during the trying journey.

## Literature

After the fall of Rome, one of the most remarkable of all Spain's literary figures was the bishop of Sevilla, San Isidoro, whose works were classic texts for over a millennium, see box, page 63.

The extraordinary life of Miguel de Cervantes (1547-1616) marks the start of a rich period of Spanish literature. *Don Quijote* came out in serial form in 1606 and is rightly considered one of the finest novels ever written; it's certainly the widest-read Spanish work. Cervantes spent plenty of time in Andalucía and some of his *Novelas Ejemplares* are short stories set in Sevilla.

The Sevillian, Lope de Rueda (1505-1565), was in many ways Spain's first playwright. He wrote comedies and paved the way for the explosion of Spanish drama under the big three – Lope de Vega, Tirso de la Molina and Calderón de la Barca – when public theatres opened in the early 17th century.

The 18th century was not such a rich period for Andalucían or Spanish writing but in the 19th century the *costumbrista* movement (see page 80) produced several fine works, among them *La Gaviota* (the Seagull), by Fernán Caballero, who was actually a Sevilla-raised woman named Cecilia Böhl von Faber, and *Escenas Andaluzas* (Andalucían Scenes), by Serafín Estébanez Calderón. Gustavo Adolfo

Bécquer, who was born in Sevilla, died young having published a famous series of legends and just one volume of poetry, popular, yearning works about love.

At the end of the 19th century, Spain lost the last of its colonial possessions after revolts and a war with the USA. This event, known as the Disaster, had a profound impact on the nation and its date 1898 gave its name to a generation of writers and artists. This group sought to express what Spain was and had been and to achieve new perspectives for the 20th century. One of their number was Antonio Machado (1875-1939), one of Spain's greatest poets; see box, page 81.

The Generation of 27 was a loose grouping of artists and writers. Sevillian poets associated with this movement include the neo-romantic Luis Cernuda (1902-1963) and Vicente Aleixandre (1898-1984), winner of the 1977 Nobel Prize for his surrealist-influenced free verse.

## Music and dance

### Flamenco

Few things symbolize the mysteries of Andalucía like flamenco but, as with the region itself, much has been written that is over-romanticized, patronizing or just plain untrue. Like bullfighting, flamenco as we know it is a fairly young art, having basically developed in the 19th century. It is constantly evolving and there have been significant changes in its performance in the last century, which makes the search for classic flamenco a bit of a wild goose chase. Rather, the element to search for is authentic emotion and, beyond this, *duende*, an undefinable passion that carries singer and watchers away in a whirlwind of raw feeling, with a devil-may-care sneer at destiny.

Though there have been many excellent *payo* flamenco artists, its history is primarily a gypsy one. It was developed among the gypsy population in the Sevilla and Cádiz area but clearly includes elements of cultures encountered further away.

Flamenco consists of three basic components: *el cante* (the song), *el toque* (the guitar) and *el baile* (the dance). In addition, *el jaleo* provides percussion sounds through shouts, clicking fingers, clapping and footwork (and, less traditionally, castanets). Flamenco can be divided into four basic types: *tonás*, *siguiriyas*, *soleá* and *tangos*, which are characterized by their *comps* or form, rhythm and accentuation and are either *cante jondo* (emotionally deep)/*cante grande* (big) or *cante ligero* (lighter)/*cante chico* (small). Related to flamenco, but not in a pure form, are *sevillanas*, danced till you drop at Feria.

For a foreigner, perhaps the classic image of flamenco is a woman in a theatrical dress clicking castanets. A more authentic image is of a singer and guitarist, both sitting rather disconsolately on ramshackle chairs, or perhaps on a wooden box to tap out a rhythm. The singer and the guitarist work together, sensing the mood of the other and improvising. A beat is provided by clapping of hands or tapping of feet. If there's a dancer, he or she will lock into the mood of the others and vice versa. The dancing is stop-start, frenetic: the flamenco can reach crescendoes of frightening intensity when it seems the singer will have a stroke, the dancer is about to commit murder, and the guitarist may never find it back to the world of the sane. These outbursts of passion are seen to their fullest in *cante jondo*, the deepest and saddest form of flamenco.

After going through a moribund period during the mid-20th century, flamenco was revived by such artists as Paco de Lucía, and the gaunt, heroin-addicted genius Camarón de la Isla, while the flamenco theatre of Joaquín Cortés put purists' noses firmly out of joint but achieved worldwide popularity. More recently, Diego 'El Cigala' carries on Camarón's angst-ridden tradition.

# Religion

The history of Spain and the history of the Spanish Catholic church are barely separable but, in 1978, Article 16 of the new constitution declared that Spain was now a nation without an official religion, less than a decade after Franco's right hand man, Admiral Luis Carrero Blanco, had declared that "Spain is Catholic or she is nothing".

From the sixth-century writings of San Isidoro (see box, page 63) onwards, the destiny of Spain was a specifically Catholic one. The *Reconquista* was a territorial war inspired by holy zeal, Jews and Moors were expelled in the quest for pure Catholic blood, the Inquisition demonstrated the young nation's religious insecurities and paranoias and Felipe II bled Spain dry pursuing futile wars in a vain attempt to protect his beloved Church from the spread of Protestantism. Much of the strife of the 1800s was caused by groups attempting to end or defend the power of the church, while in the 20th century the fall of the Second Republic and the Civil War was engendered to a large extent by the provocatively anticlerical actions of the leftists.

Faced with a census form, a massive 94% of Spaniards claim to be Catholics, but less than a third of them cut regular figures in the parish church. Although regular churchgoing is increasingly confined to an aged (mostly female) segment of society and seminaries struggle to produce enough priests to stock churches, it's not the whole picture. *Romerías* (religious processions to rural chapels and sites) and religious fiestas are well attended and places of pilgrimage, usually chapels housing venerated statues of the Virgin, are flooded with Spanish visitors during the summer months. Very few weddings are conducted away from the church's bosom and, come Easter, a big percentage of the male population of some towns participates in solemn processions of religious *cofradías* (brotherhoods), most famously in Sevilla. Nevertheless, the church plays an increasingly minor role in most Spaniards' lives, especially those of those born after the return to democracy.

# Practicalities
## Seville

# **Getting** there

## Air

There are numerous options for reaching Sevilla. As well as Sevilla airport, you can fly into Málaga, Jerez de la Frontera or Gibraltar.

Charter flights are cheaper and are run by package holiday firms. You can find bargains through travel agencies or online. The drawback of these flights is that they usually have a fixed return flight, often only a week or a fortnight later, and they frequently depart at antisocial hours. An upside is that charter flights operate from many regional airports.

Before booking, it's worth doing a bit of online research. Three of the best search engines for flight comparisons are www.opodo.com, www.skyscanner.com and www.kayak.com, which compare prices from a range of agencies. To keep up to date with the ever-changing routes available, sites like www.flightmapper.net are handy. Flightchecker (http://flightchecker.moneysavingexpert.com) is handy for checking multiple dates for budget airline deals.

### Flights from the UK
Competition has benefited travellers in recent years. Budget operators have taken a significant slice of the market and forced other airlines to compete.

**Budget** There are numerous budget connections from the UK to Sevilla and Málaga. Easyjet and Ryanair fly from over a dozen UK airports, while other budget airlines running various routes from the UK include Flybe, Vueling, Norwegian, Jet2, Thomson and Monarch.

**Charter** There are numerous charter flights to Málaga from many British and Irish airports. Avro ⓘ www.avro.co.uk, Thomas Cook ⓘ www.thomascook.com, and Thomson ⓘ www.thomson.co.uk, are some of the best charter flight providers, but it's also worth checking the travel pages of newspapers for cheap deals. The website www.flightsdirect.com is also a good tool to search for charter flights.

**Non-budget flights** Málaga again has the most scheduled flights, with several airlines including Iberia and British Airways flying direct from London airports and a few other UK cities. From London, there are daily direct flights to Sevilla.

### Flights from the rest of Europe
There are numerous budget airlines operating from European and Spanish cities to Málaga and Sevilla.

Numerous charter flights operate to Málaga from Germany, Scandinavia, France, the Netherlands and Belgium.

There are non-stop flights to Málaga with non-budget airlines from many major European cities. There are daily non-stop flights to Sevilla from a few European

**TRAVEL TIP**

**Packing for Seville**

Spain is a modern European country, and you can buy almost everything you'll need here; packing light is the way to go. A GPS device is handy for navigating and a European adaptor (plug a double adaptor into it) is a must for recharging electrical goods (see page 101).

capitals. Flying from these or other western European cities via Madrid or Barcelona usually costs about the same.

### Flights from North America and Canada
**Delta** fly direct from New York to Málaga, while there are fortnightly charter flights from Montreal and Toronto with **Air Transat**. Otherwise, you'll have to connect via Madrid, Barcelona, Lisbon, London or another European city to Andalucían airports. Although sometimes you'll pay little extra to Andalucía than the Madrid flight, you can often save considerably by flying to Madrid and getting the bus down south or book a domestic connection on the local no-frills airline **Vueling** ⓘ *www.vueling.com*, or **Ryanair** ⓘ *www.ryanair.com*.

### Flights from Australia and New Zealand
There are no direct flights to Spain from Australia or New Zealand; the cheapest and quickest way is to connect via Frankfurt, Paris or London. It might turn out cheaper to book the Europe–Spain leg separately via a budget operator.

## Road

**Bus**
**Eurolines** ⓘ *T01582-404511, www.eurolines.com*, runs several buses from major European cities to Sevilla, but you won't get there cheaper than a flight.

**Car and sea**
It's a long haul to Sevilla by road if you're not already in the peninsula. From the UK, you have two options if you want to take the car: take a ferry to northern Spain (www.brittany-ferries.co.uk), or cross the Channel to France and then drive down. The former option is much more expensive; it would usually work out far cheaper to fly to Sevilla and hire a car once you get there. For competitive fares by sea to France and Spain, check with **Ferrysavers** ⓘ *www.ferrysavers.com*, or **Direct Ferries** ⓘ *www.directferries.com*.

Sevilla is about 2000 km from London by road; a dedicated drive will get you there in 20-24 driving hours. By far the fastest route is to head down the west coast of France and to Burgos via San Sebastián. From here, head for Salamanca then south.

## Train

Unless you've got a rail pass, love train travel or aren't too keen on planes, forget about getting to Sevilla by train from anywhere further than France; you'll save no money over the plane fare and use up days of time better spent in tapas bars. You'll have to connect via either Barcelona or Madrid. Getting to Madrid/Barcelona from London takes about a day using **Eurostar** ⓘ *www.eurostar.com, £100-250 return to Paris, and another €130 or more return to reach Madrid/Barcelona from there*. Using the train/Channel ferry combination will more or less halve the cost and double the time to Paris.

If you are planning the train journey, **Voyages**-SNCF ⓘ *www.voyages-sncf.com*, is a useful company. **RENFE**, Spain's rail network, has online timetables at www.renfe.com. Best of all is the extremely useful www.seat61.com.

# **Getting** around

## Road

### Bus

Buses are the staple of Spanish public transport. Services between major cities are fast, frequent, reliable and fairly cheap; the six-hour trip from Madrid to Sevilla, for example, costs €23. When buying a ticket, always check how long the journey will take, as the odd bus will be an 'all stations to' job, calling in at villages that seem surprised to even see it.

Most towns and cities have a single terminal, the *estación de autobuses*. Buy your tickets at the relevant window; if there isn't one, buy it from the driver. Superior classes may cost up to 60% more but offer lounge access and onboard service. Newer buses in all classes may offer Wi-Fi, personal entertainment system and sockets. Most tickets will have an *asiento* (seat number) on them; ask when buying the ticket if you prefer a *ventana* (window) or *pasillo* (aisle) seat. Some of the companies allow booking online or by phone. If you're travelling at busy times (particularly a fiesta or national holiday) always book the bus ticket in advance.

Rural bus services are slower, less frequent and more difficult to coordinate.

All bus services are reduced on Sundays and, to a lesser extent, on Saturdays; some services don't run at all on weekends.

### Car

**Roads and motorways** The roads in Sevilla are good, excellent in many parts. While driving isn't as sedate as in parts of northern Europe, it's generally pretty good and you'll have few problems.

There are two types of motorway in Spain, *autovías* and *autopistas*; for drivers, they are little different. They are signposted in blue and may have tolls payable, in which case there'll be a red warning circle on the blue sign when you're entering the motorway. Tolls are generally reasonable; the quality of motorway is generally excellent. The speed limit on motorways is 120 kph, though it is scheduled to rise to 130 kph on some stretches.

*Rutas Nacionales* form the backbone of the country's road network. Centrally administered, they vary wildly in quality. Typically, they are choked with traffic backed up behind trucks, and there are few stretches of dual carriageway. Driving at siesta time is a good idea if you're going to be on a busy stretch. *Rutas Nacionales* are marked with a red N followed by a number. The speed limit is 100 kph outside built-up areas, as it is for secondary roads, which are usually marked with an A (Andalucía), or C (*comarcal*, or local) prefix.

In urban areas, the speed limit is 50 kph. City driving can be confusing, with signposting generally poor and traffic heavy; it's worth using a Satnav or printing off the directions that your hotel may send you with a reservation. In some towns and cities, many of the hotels are officially signposted, making things easier.

Larger cities may have their historic quarter blocked off by barriers; if your hotel lies within these, ring the buzzer and say the name of the hotel, and the barriers will open. Other cities enforce restrictions by camera, so you'll have to give your number plate details to the hotel so they can register it.

Police are increasingly enforcing speed limits in Spain, and foreign drivers are liable to a large on-the-spot fine. Drivers can also be punished for not carrying two red warning triangles to place on the road in case of breakdown, a bulb-replacement kit and a fluorescent green waistcoat to wear if you break down by the side of the road. Drink driving is being cracked down on; the limit is 0.5 g/l of blood, a little lower than the equivalent in the UK, for example.

**Parking**  Parking is a problem in nearly every town and city in Sevilla province. Red or yellow lines on the side of the street mean no parking. Blue or white lines mean that some restrictions are in place; a sign will indicate what these are (typically it means that the parking is metered). Parking meters can usually only be dosed up for a maximum of two hours, but they take a siesta at lunchtime too. Print the ticket off and display it in the car. If you overstay and get fined, you can pay it off for minimal cost at the machine if you do it within an hour of the fine being issued. Parking fines are never pursued for foreign vehicles, but if it's a hire car you'll likely be liable for it. Underground car parks are common, but pricey; €15-20 a day is normal. The website www.parkopedia.es is useful for locating underground car parks and comparing their rates.

**Documentation**  To drive in Spain, you'll need a full driving licence from your home country. This applies to virtually all foreign nationals but, in practice, if you're from an 'unusual' country, consider an International Driving Licence or official translation of your licence into Spanish.

Liability insurance is required for every car driven in Spain and you must carry proof of it. If bringing your own car, check carefully with your insurers that you're covered and get a certificate (green card).

**Car hire**  Hiring a car is easy and cheap. The major multinationals have offices at all large towns and airports. Prices start at around €150 per week for a small car with unlimited mileage. You'll need a credit card and most agencies will either not accept under-25s or demand a surcharge. By far the cheapest place to hire a car is Málaga, where even at the airport there are competitive rates. With the bigger companies, it's always cheaper to book over the internet. The best way to look for a deal is using a price-comparison website like www.kayak.com. Drop-offs in other cities, which used to be ridiculously punitive, are now often much more affordable.

There are often hidden charges, the most common being compulsory purchase of a tank of petrol at an overpriced rate. You then have to return the car with the tank empty.

## Cycling and motorcycling

Motorcycling is a good way to enjoy Sevilla and there are few difficulties to trouble the biker; bike shops and mechanics are relatively common. There are comparatively few outlets for motorcycle hire.

Cycling presents a curious contrast; Spaniards are mad for the competitive sport, but essentially disinterested in cycling as a means of transport, though local governments are trying to encourage it with new bike lanes and free borrowable bikes in cities. Thus there are plenty of cycling shops but few cycle-friendly features on the roads. Taking your own bike to Sevilla is well worth the effort as most airlines are happy to accept them, providing they come within your baggage allowance. Bikes can be taken on the train, but have to travel in the guard's van and must be registered.

## Hitchhiking

Hitchhiking is fairly easy in Spain, although not much practised. The police aren't too keen on it, but with sensible placement and a clearly written sign, you'll usually get a lift without a problem, particularly in rural areas, where, in the absence of bus services, it's a more common way for locals to get about.

## Taxi and bus

Sevilla city and the provincial towns have their sights closely packed into the centre, so you won't find local buses particularly necessary. There's a fairly comprehensive network in most towns, though; the travel text indicates where they come in handy. Taxis are a good option; the minimum charge is around €2.50 in most places (it increases slightly at night and on Sundays). A taxi is available if its green light is lit; hail one on the street, call, or ask for the nearest *parada de taxis* (rank). If you're using a cab to get to somewhere beyond the city limits, there are fixed tariffs.

## Train

The Spanish national rail network, **RENFE** ⓘ *T902-240202 (English-speaking operators), www.renfe.com for timetables and tickets*, is, thanks to its growing network of high-speed trains, a useful option. AVE trains run from Madrid to Sevilla and, though expensive, cover this large distance impressively quickly and reliably. Elsewhere though, you'll find the bus is often quicker and cheaper.

Prices vary significantly according to the type of service you are using. The standard high-speed intercity service is called *Talgo*, while other intercity services are labelled *Altaria*, *Intercity*, *Diurno* and *Estrella* (overnight). Slower local trains are called *regionales*. Alvia is a mixed AVE-Talgo service.

It's always worth buying a ticket in advance for long-distance travel, as trains are often full. The best option is to buy them via the website, which sometimes offers advance purchase discounts. The website is notoriously unreliable, with not all services appearing, and a clunky mechanism for finding connections. You can print out the ticket yourself, or print it at a railway station using the reservation code. If buying your ticket at the station, allow plenty of time for queuing. Ticket windows are labelled *venta anticipada* (in advance) and *venta inmediata* (six hours or less before the journey).

All Spanish trains are non-smoking. The faster trains will have a first-class (*preferente*) and second-class sections as well as a cafeteria. First class costs about 30% more than standard and can be a worthwhile deal on a crowded long journey. Families and groups can take advantage of the cheap 'mesa' tickets, where you reserve four seats around a table. Buying a return ticket is 10% to 20% cheaper than two singles, but you qualify for this discount even if you buy the return leg later (but not on every service).

An **ISIC student card** or **youth card** grants a discount of 20% to 25% on train services. If you're using a European railpass, be aware that you'll still have to make a reservation on Spanish trains and pay the small reservation fee (which covers your insurance). If you have turned 60, it's worth paying €6 for a Tarjeta Dorada, a seniors' card that gets you a discount of 40% on trains from Monday to Thursday, and 25% at other times.

## Maps

A useful website for route planning is www.guiarepsol.com. Car hire companies have Satnavs available, though they cost a hefty supplement.

# **Where** to stay

The standard of accommodation in Sevilla is very high; even the most modest of *pensiones* is usually very clean and respectable. At time of writing, for Spain the website www.booking.com is by far the most comprehensive and has the best rates; www.hotels.com and www.laterooms.com have some good deals too. If you're booking accommodation not listed in this guide, always be sure to check the location if that's important to you – it's easy to find yourself a 15-minute cab ride from town.

Environmental issues are an individual's responsibility, and the type of holiday you choose has a direct impact on the future of the region. Opting for more sustainable tourism choices – picking a *casa rural* in a traditional village and eating in restaurants serving locally sourced food rather than staying in the four-star multinational hotel – has a small but significant knock-on effect. Don't be afraid to ask questions about environmental policy before making a hotel or *casa rural* booking.

## Types of accommodation

*Alojamientos* (places to stay), are divided into two main categories; the distinctions between them are in an arcane series of regulations devised by the government.

### Hotels, hostales and pensiones
*Hoteles* (marked H or HR) are graded from one to five stars and occupy their own building, which distinguishes them from many *hostales* (Hs or HsR), which go from one to two stars. The *hostal* category includes *pensiones*, the standard budget option, typically family-run and occupying a floor of an apartment building. The standard for the price paid is normally excellent, and they're nearly all spotless. Spanish traditions of hospitality are alive and well; check-out time is almost uniformly a very civilized midday.

A great number of Spanish hotels are well equipped but characterless chain business places (big players include NH ⓘ *www.nh-hoteles.es*,

---

## **Price** codes

| Where to stay | |
|---|---|
| €€€€ | over €170 |
| €€€ | €110-170 |
| €€ | €60-110 |
| € | under €60 |

A standard double/twin room in high season.

| Restaurants | |
|---|---|
| €€€ | over €30 |
| €€ | €15-30 |
| € | under €15 |

A two-course meal (or two average *raciones*) for one person, without drinks.

Husa ⓘ *www.husa.es*, AC/Marriott ⓘ *www.marriott.com*, Tryp/SolMelia ⓘ *www. solmelia.com*, and Riu ⓘ *www.riu.com*), and can be found in and around the centre of Sevilla city. This guide has expressly minimized these in the listings, preferring to concentrate on more atmospheric options.

## Casas rurales

An excellent option if you've got your own transport are the networks of rural houses, called *casas rurales*. Although these are under a different classification system, the standard is often as high as any country hotel. The best of them are traditional farmhouses or characterful village cottages. Some are available only to rent out whole (often for a minimum of three days), while others offer rooms on a nightly basis. Rates tend to be excellent compared to hotels. While many are listed in the text, there are huge numbers of them. Local tourist offices will have details; the tourist board lists a good selection on www.andalucia.org.

## Youth hostels

There's a network of *albergues* (youth hostels), which are listed at www.inturjoven. com. These are institutional and often group-booked. Funding issues mean that many now open only seasonally. Major cities have backpacker hostels.

## Campsites

Most campsites are set up as well-equipped holiday villages for families; some are open only in summer. While the facilities are good, they get extremely busy in peak season. Many have cabins or bungalows available, ranging from simple huts to houses with fully equipped kitchens and bathrooms. In other areas, camping, unless specifically prohibited, is a matter of common sense. Don't camp where you're not allowed to; prohibitions are usually there for a good reason. Fire danger can be high in summer, so respect local regulations.

## Prices

Price codes refer to a standard double or twin room, inclusive of VAT. The rates are generally for high season (March-May in Sevilla city). Occasionally, an area or town will have a short period when prices are hugely exaggerated; this is usually due to a festival.

Breakfast is often included in the price at small intimate hotels, but rarely at the grander places, who tend to charge a fortune. Normally only the more expensive hotels have parking, and they always charge for it, normally around €10-25 per day.

All registered accommodation charge a 10% value added tax; this is usually included in the price and may be waived if you pay cash. If you have any problems, a last resort is to ask for the *libro de reclamaciones* (complaints book), an official document that, like stepping on cracks in the pavement, means uncertain but definitely horrible consequences for the hotel if anything is written in it. Be aware that you must also take a copy to the local police station for the complaint to be registered.

# **Food** & drink

In no country in the world are culture and society as intimately connected with eating and drinking as in Spain, and in Sevilla, the spiritual home of tapas, this is even more the case.

**Food** → *See page 114 for a glossary of food.*

Cooking in Sevilla is characterized by an abundance of fresh ingredients, generally consecrated with the chef's holy trinity of garlic, peppers and local olive oil.

Spaniards eat little for breakfast and, apart from hotels in touristy places, you're unlikely to find anything beyond a *tostada* (large piece of toasted bread spread with olive oil, tomato and garlic, pâté or jam) or a pastry to go with your coffee. A common breakfast or afternoon snack are *churros*, fried dough sticks typically dipped in hot chocolate.

Lunch is the main meal and is nearly always a filling affair with three courses. Most places open for lunch at about 1300, and take last orders at 1500 or 1530, although at weekends this can extend. Lunchtime is the cheapest time to eat if you opt for the ubiquitous *menú del día*, usually a set three-course meal that includes wine or soft drink, typically costing €10 to €16. Dinner and/or evening tapas time is from around 2100 to midnight. It's not much fun sitting alone in a restaurant so try and adapt to the local hours; it may feel strange dining so late, but you'll miss out on a lot of atmosphere if you don't. If a place is open for lunch at noon, or dinner at 1900, it's likely to be a tourist trap.

## Types of eateries

The great joy of eating out in Sevilla is going for tapas. This word refers to bar food, served in saucer-sized tapa portions typically costing €1.50-3. Tapas are available at lunchtime, but the classic time to eat them is in the evening. To do tapas the Andalucían way don't order more than a couple at each place, taste each others' dishes, and stand at the bar. Locals know what the specialities of each bar are; if there's a daily special, order that. Also available are *raciones*, substantial meal-sized plates of the same fare, which also come in halves, *medias raciones*. Both are good for sharing. Considering these, the distinction between restaurants and tapas bars more or less disappears, as in the latter you can usually sit down at a table to order your *raciones*, effectively turning the experience into a meal.

Other types of eateries include a *freiduría*, a takeaway specializing in fried fish, while a *marisquería* is a classier type of seafood restaurant. In rural areas, look out for *ventas*, roadside eateries that often have a long history of feeding the passing muleteers with generous, hearty and cheap portions. The more cars and trucks outside, the better it will be. In Sevilla city, North African-style teahouses, *teterías*, are popular.

## Vegetarian food

Vegetarians in Sevilla won't be spoiled for choice, but at least what there is tends to be good. There are few dedicated vegetarian restaurants and many restaurants won't have a vegetarian main course on offer, although the existence of tapas, *raciones* and salads makes this less of a burden than it might be. You'll have to specify *soy vegetariano/a* (I am a vegetarian), but ask what dishes contain, as ham, fish and even chicken are often considered suitable vegetarian fare. Vegans will have a tougher time. What doesn't have meat nearly always contains cheese or egg. Better restaurants, particularly in Sevilla city, will be happy to prepare something, but otherwise stick to very simple dishes.

## On the menu

Typical starters include *gazpacho* (a cold summer tomato soup flavoured with garlic, olive oil and peppers; *salmorejo* is a thicker version from Córdoba), *ensalada mixta* (mixed salad based on lettuce, tomatoes, tuna and more), or paella.

Main courses will usually be either meat or fish and are rarely served with any accompaniment beyond chips. Beef is common; the better steaks such as *solomillo* or *entrecot* are usually superbly tender. Spaniards tend to eat them fairly rare (*poco hecho*; ask for *al punto* for medium rare or *bien hecho* for well done). Pork is also widespread; *solomillo de cerdo*, *secreto*, *pluma* and *lomo* are all tasty cuts. Innards are popular: *callos* (tripe), *mollejas* (sweetbreads) and *morcilla* (black pudding) are excellent, if acquired, tastes.

Seafood is the pride of Andalucía. The region is famous for its *pescaíto frito* (fried fish) which typically consists of small fry such as whitebait in batter. Shellfish include *mejillones* (mussels), *gambas* (prawns) and *coquillas* (cockles). *Calamares* (calamari), *sepia* or *choco* (cuttlefish) and *chipirones* (small squid) are common, and you'll sometimes see *pulpo* (octopus). Among the vertebrates, *sardinas* (sardines), *dorada* (gilthead bream), *rape* (monkfish) and *pez espada* (swordfish) are all usually excellent.

Signature tapas dishes vary from bar to bar and from province to province, and part of the delight of Sevilla comes trying regional specialities. Ubiquitous are *jamón* (cured ham; the best, *ibérico*, comes from black-footed acorn-eating porkers that roam the woods of Huelva province and Extremadura) and *queso* (usually the hard salty *manchego* from Castilla-la Mancha). *Gambas* (prawns) are usually on the tapas list; the best and priciest are from Huelva.

Desserts focus on the sweet and milky. *Flan* (a sort of crème caramel) is ubiquitous; great when *casero* (home-made), but often out of a plastic tub. *Natillas* are a similar but more liquid version, while Moorish-style pastries are also specialities of some areas.

## Drink

### Alcoholic drinks

In good Catholic fashion, wine is the blood of Spain. It's the standard accompaniment to meals, but also features prominently in bars. *Tinto* is red (if you just order *vino* this is what you'll get), *blanco* is white and rosé is *rosado*.

A well-regulated system of *denominaciones de origen* (DO), similar to the French *appelation d'origine contrôlée*, has lifted the quality and reputation of Spanish wines. While the daddy in terms of production and popularity is still Rioja, regions such as the Ribera del Duero, Rueda, Bierzo, Jumilla, Priorat and Valdepeñas have achieved worldwide recognition. The words *crianza*, *reserva* and *gran reserva* refer to the length and nature of the ageing process.

One of the joys of Spain, though, is the rest of the wine. Order a *menú del día* at a cheap restaurant and you'll be unceremoniously served a cheap bottle of local red. Wine snobbery can leave by the back door at this point: it may be cold, but you'll find it refreshing; it may be acidic, but once the olive-oil laden food arrives, you'll be glad of it. People add water to it if they feel like it, or *gaseosa* (lemonade) or cola (for the party drink *calimocho*).

Andalucía produces several table wines of this sort. The whites of the Condado region in eastern Huelva province and those from nearby Cádiz are simple seafood companions. Bartenders throughout Andalucía tend to assume that tourists only want Rioja, so be sure to specify *vino corriente* (or *vino de la zona*) if you want to try the local stuff. As a general rule, only bars that serve food serve wine; most *pubs* and *discotecas* won't have it. Cheaper red wine is often served cold, a refreshing alternative in summer. *Tinto de verano* is a summery mix of red wine and lemonade, often with fruit added, while the stronger *sangría* adds healthy measures of sherry and sometimes spirits to the mix. The real vinous fame of the region comes, of course, from its fortified wines; sherries and others.

Beer is mostly lager, usually reasonably strong, fairly gassy, cold and good. Sweetish Cruzcampo from Sevilla is found throughout the region; other local brews include San Miguel, named after the archangel and brewed in Málaga, and Alhambra from Granada. A *caña* or *tubo* is a glass of draught beer, while just specifying *cerveza* usually gets you a bottle, otherwise known as a *botellín*. Many people order their beer *con gas* (half beer and half fizzy sweet water) or *con limón* (half lemonade, also called a *clara*).

*Vermut* (vermouth) is a popular pre-lunch aperitif. Many bars make their own vermouth by adding various herbs and fruits and letting it sit in barrels.

After dinner it's time for a *copa*. People relax over a whisky or a brandy, or hit the *cubatas* (mixed drinks); gin and tonic, rum and coke, whisky and coke are the most popular. Spirits are free-poured and large.

When ordering a spirit, you'll be expected to choose which brand you want; the range of, particularly, gins, is extraordinary. There's always a good selection of rum (*ron*) and blended whisky available too. *Chupitos* are short drinks often served in shot-glasses.

### Non-alcoholic drinks

*Zumo* (fruit juice) is normally bottled; *mosto* (grape juice, really pre-fermented wine) is a popular soft drink in bars. All bars serve alcohol-free beer (*cerveza sin alcohol*). *Horchata* is a summer drink, a sort of milkshake made from tiger nuts. *Agua* (water) comes *con* (with) or *sin* (without) *gas*. The tap water is totally safe.

*Café* (coffee) is excellent and strong. *Solo* is black, served espresso style. Order *americano* if you want a long black, *cortado* if you want a dash of milk, or *con leche* for about half milk. *Té* (tea) is served without milk unless you ask; herbal teas (*infusiones*) are common, especially chamomile (*manzanilla*; don't confuse with the sherry of the same name) and mint (*menta poleo*).

# Essentials A-Z

## Accidents and emergencies

**General emergencies** 112.

## Children

Kids are kings in Spain and it's one of the easiest places to take them along on holiday. Children socialize with their parents from an early age and you'll see them eating in restaurants and out in bars well after midnight. Outdoor summer life and pedestrianized areas of cities make for a stress-free time for both you and the kids.

Spaniards are friendly and accommodating towards children and you'll undoubtedly get treated better with them than without them, except perhaps in the most expensive restaurants and hotels. Few places, however, are equipped with highchairs or baby-changing facilities. Children are expected to eat the same sort of things as their parents, although you'll sometimes see a *menú infantil* at a restaurant, which typically has simpler dishes and smaller portions. Many of the newer museums are hands-on. Spanish campsites are well set up; the larger ones often with child-minding facilities.

The cut-off age for children paying half or being free on public transport and in tourist attractions varies widely. RENFE trains let under-4s on free and offer discounts of around 50% for 4-12 year-olds. Most car-rental companies have child seats available, but it's wise to book these in advance, particularly in summer.

Bear in mind that Sevilla can get unbearably hot in the summer.

## Customs and duty free

Non-EU citizens are allowed to import 1 litre of spirits, 2 litres of wine and 200 cigarettes or 250 g of tobacco or 50 cigars. EU citizens are theoretically limited by personal use only.

## Disabled travellers

Spain isn't the best equipped of countries in terms of disabled travel, but things are improving rapidly. By law, all new public buildings have to have full disabled access and facilities, but disabled toilets are rare elsewhere. Facilities generally are significantly better in Andalucía than in the rest of the country.

Most trains and stations are wheelchair friendly to some degree, as are many urban buses, but intercity buses are largely not accessible. **Hertz** in Málaga and Sevilla have a small range of cars set up with hand controls, but be sure to book them well in advance. Nearly all underground and municipal car parks have lifts and disabled spaces, as do many museums, castles, etc.

An invaluable resource for finding a bed are the regional accommodation lists, available from tourist offices and the www.andalucia.org website. Most of these include a disabled-access criterion. Many *hostales* are in buildings with ramps and lifts, but there are many that are not, and the lifts can be very small. Nearly all paradores and chain hotels are fully accessible by wheelchair, as is any accommodation built since 1995, but it's best to phone. Be sure to check details as many hotels' claims are well intentioned but not fully thought through.

While major cities are relatively straightforward, smaller towns and villages frequently have uneven footpaths, steep streets (often cobbled) and little, if any, disabled infrastructure.

### Useful contacts
**Confederación Nacional de Sordos de España (CNSE)**, www.cnse.es, has links to local associations for the deaf.
**Global Access**, www.globalaccessnews.com, has regular reports from disabled travellers as well as links to other sites.
**ONCE**, www.once.es. The blind are well catered for as a result of the efforts of ONCE, the national organization for the blind, which runs a lucrative daily lottery. It can provide information on accessible attractions for blind travellers.

## Electricity

230V. A round 2-pin plug is used (European standard).

## Embassies and consulates

For a list of Spanish embassies abroad, see http://embassy.goabroad.com.

## Festivals and public holidays

### Festivals
As well as Sevilla's famous Semana Santa and Feria de Abril celebrations (see boxes, pages 18 and 26), in Sep/Oct the Bienal de Flamenco is held every even-numbered year. The most respected names in flamenco perform here, with more than 600 artists taking part. Check dates at www.labienal.com.

Even the smallest village in Sevilla has a fiesta and many have several. Although mostly nominally religious featuring a mass and procession or two, they also offer live music, bullfights, competitions and fireworks. A feature of many are *gigantes y cabezudos*, huge-headed papier mâché figures based on historical personages who parade the streets. In many villages there's a *Moros y Cristianos* festival, which recreates a Reconquista battle with colourful costumes.

Most fiestas are in summer; expect some trouble finding accommodation. Details of the major town fiestas can be found in the travel text. National holidays and *puentes* (long weekends) can be difficult times to travel; it's important to reserve tickets in advance.

### Public holidays
**1 Jan Año Nuevo**, New Year's Day.
**6 Jan Reyes Magos/Epifanía**, Epiphany, when Christmas presents are given.
**28 Feb Andalucía day.**
**Easter Jueves Santo, Viernes Santo, Día de Pascua** (Maundy Thu, Good Fri, Easter Sun).
**1 May Fiesta del Trabajo** (Labour Day).
**24 Jun Fiesta de San Juan** (Feast of St John and name-day of the king Juan Carlos I).
**25 Jul Día del Apostol Santiago**, Feast of St James.
**15 Aug Asunción**, Feast of the Assumption.
**12 Oct Día de la Hispanidad**, Spanish National Day (Columbus Day, Feast of the Virgin of the Pillar).
**1 Nov Todos los Santos**, All Saints' Day.
**6 Dec El Día de la Constitución Española**, Constitution Day.
**8 Dec Inmaculada Concepción**, Feast of the Immaculate Conception.
**25 Dec Navidad**, Christmas Day.

## Gay and lesbian travellers

Homosexuality is legal, as is gay marriage, though it's just the sort of thing the incumbent Partido Popular would like to revoke. There are different levels of tolerance and open-mindedness towards gays and lesbians in Andalucía. In Sevilla there's a substantial amount of gay life, although not on a par with Barcelona or Madrid. In smaller places, however, it can be a different story, and a couple walking hand-in-hand will likely be greeted with incredulous stares, although rarely anything worse.

### Useful contacts
**COLEGA**, www.colegaweb.org. A gay and lesbian association with an office in Sevilla.
**Shangay/Shanguide**, www.shangay.com, is a useful magazine with reviews, events, information and city-by-city listings for the whole country.

### Useful websites
**www.damron.com** Subscription listings and travel info.

## Health

Medical facilities in Sevilla are very good. However, EU citizens should make sure they have the **European Health Insurance Card** (EHIC) to prove reciprocal rights to medical care. These are available free of charge in the UK from the Department of Health (www.dh.gov.uk) or post offices.

**Non-EU citizens** should consider travel insurance to cover emergency and routine medical needs; be sure that it covers any sports or activities you may do. Check for reciprocal cover with your private or public health scheme first.

**Water** is safe to drink. The **sun** in southern Spain can be harsh, so take precautions to avoid heat exhaustion and sunburn.

Many medications that require a prescription in other countries are available over the counter at pharmacies in Spain. Pharmacists are highly trained and usually speak some English. In medium-sized towns and Sevilla city, at least one pharmacy is open 24 hrs; this is performed on a rota system (posted in the window of all pharmacies and listed in local newspapers).

No vaccinations are needed.

## Insurance

Insurance is a good idea to cover you for theft. In the unlucky event of theft, you'll have to make a report at the local police station within 24 hrs and obtain a *denuncia* (report) to show your insurers. See above for health cover for EU citizens.

## Internet

Cyber cafés are increasingly rare in Spain, though you'll still find them in Sevilla city. Other places that often offer access are *locutorios* (call shops), which are common in areas with a high immigrant population. Most accommodation and an increasing number of cafés and restaurants offer Wi-Fi. Internet places tend to appear and disappear rapidly, so we have minimized listings in this guide; ask the tourist information office for the latest place to get online. Mobile phone providers offer pay-as-you-go data SIM cards and USB modems at a reasonable rate. Roaming charges within the EU are set to be abolished in late 2015, so mobile data usage will cost EU residents no more in Sevilla than it would in your home country.

## Language

Everyone in Sevilla speaks Spanish, known either as *castellano* or *español*, and it's a huge help to know some. The local accent, *andaluz*, is characterized by dropping consonants left, right and centre, thus *dos tapas* tends to be pronounced *dotapa*. Unlike in the rest of Spain, the letters 'c' and 'z' in words such as *cerveza* aren't pronounced 'th' (although in Cádiz province, perversely, they tend to pronounce 's' with that sound).

Most young people know some English, and standards are rising fast, but don't assume that people aged 40 or over know any at all. Spaniards are often shy to attempt to speak English. While many visitor attractions have some sort of information available in English (and to a lesser extent French and German), many don't, or have English tours only in times of high demand. Most tourist office staff will speak at least some English and there's a good range of translated information available in most places. People are used to speaking English in well-visited areas, but trying even a couple of words of Spanish is basic politeness. Small courtesies grease the wheels of everyday interaction here: greet the proprietor or waiting staff when entering a shop or bar, and say *hasta luego* when leaving. See page 110, for useful words and phrases in Spanish, and box, page 50, for language schools in Sevilla.

## Media

### Newspapers and magazines

The Spanish press is generally of a high journalistic standard. The national dailies, *El País* (still a qualitative leap ahead), *El Mundo* and the rightist *ABC*, are read throughout the country, but local papers are widely read in Sevilla. Overall circulation is low, partly because many people read newspapers provided in cafés and bars. Each major city has its own newspaper; in Sevilla, *El Correo* is one of the best. There are also 'what's on' magazines, often distributed in tourist offices or bars.

The terribly Real Madrid-biased sports dailies *Marca* and *As*, dedicated mostly to football, have a large readership that rivals any of the broadsheets. There's no tabloid press as such; the closest equivalent is the *prensa de corazón* and the gossip magazines such as *¡Hola!*, forerunner of Britain's *Hello!* English-language newspapers are widely available in kiosks in Sevilla and larger towns. Several English dailies now have European editions available on the day of publication; the same goes for major European dailies.

### Radio

Radio is big in Spain, with audience figures relatively higher than most of Europe. There's a huge range of stations, mainly on FM wavelengths, many of them broadcasting to a fairly small regional area. You'll be unlikely to get much exposure to it (beyond the top-40 music stations blaring in bars) unless you're in a car.

### TV

TV is the dominant medium in Spain, with audience figures well above most of the EU. The main channels are the state-run *TVE1*, with standard programming, and *TVE2*, with a more cultural/sporting bent alongside the private *Antena 3*, *Cuatro* and *Tele 5*, *La Sexta (6)*, and *Canal Plus*. Regional stations also draw audiences. Overall quality is low, with reality shows and lowest-common-denominator kitsch as popular here as anywhere. Cable TV is widespread, and satellite and digital have a wide market.

## Money

### Currency and exchange
For up-to-the-minute exchange rates visit www.xe.com.

In 2002, Spain switched to the euro, bidding farewell to the peseta. The euro (€) is divided into 100 *céntimos*. Euro notes are standard across the whole euro zone and come in denominations of 5, 10, 20, 50, 100, and the rarely seen 200 and 500. Coins have one standard face and one national face; all coins are, however, acceptable in all countries. The coins are slightly difficult to tell apart when you're not used to them. The coppers are 1, 2 and 5 cent pieces, the golds are 10, 20 and 50, and the silver/gold combinations are €1 and €2. The exchange rate was approximately €6 to 1000 pesetas or 166 pesetas to the euro. Some people still quote large amounts, like house prices, in pesetas.

### ATMs and banks
The best way to get money in Spain is by plastic. ATMs are plentiful and accept all the major international debit and credit cards. The Spanish bank won't charge for the transaction, though they will charge a mark-up on the exchange rate, but beware of your own bank hitting you for a hefty fee: check with them before leaving home. Even if they do, it's likely to be a better deal than changing cash over a counter.

Banks are usually open Mon-Fri (and Sat in winter) 0830-1430 and many change foreign money (sometimes only the central branch in a town will

do it). Commission rates vary widely; it's usually best to change large amounts, as there's often a minimum commission. The website www.moneysavingexpert.com has a good rundown on the most economical ways of accessing cash while travelling.

### Cost of living
Prices have soared since the euro was introduced; some basics rose by 50-80% in 3 years, and hotel and restaurant prices can even seem dear by Western European standards these days. Nevertheless, Sevilla still offers value for money, and you can get by cheaply if you forgo a few luxuries. If you're travelling as a pair, staying in cheap *pensiones*, eating a set meal at lunchtime, travelling short distances by bus or train daily, and snacking on tapas in the evenings, €65 per person per day is reasonable. If you camp and grab picnic lunches from shops, you could reduce this somewhat. In a good *hostal* or cheap hotel and using a car, €150 a day and you'll not be counting pennies; €300 per day and you'll be very comfy indeed unless you're staying in 5-star accommodation.

Accommodation is usually more expensive in summer than winter. Sevilla is noticeably pricier than elsewhere in Andalucía.

Public transport is generally cheap; intercity bus services are quick and low-priced, though the new fast trains are expensive. If you're hiring a car, Málaga is the cheapest place in Andalucía. Standard unleaded petrol is around 150 cents per litre. In some places, particularly in tourist areas, you may be charged up to 20% more to sit outside a restaurant. It's also worth checking if the 10% IVA (sales tax) is included in menu prices, especially in the more expensive restaurants; it should say on the menu.

## Opening hours

**Business hours** Mon-Fri 1000-1400, 1700-2000; Sat 1000-1400. **Banks** Mon-Fri, plus sometimes Sat in winter, 0830-1430. **Government offices** Mornings only.

## Post

The Spanish post is still notoriously inefficient and slow by European standards. *Correos* (post offices) generally open Mon-Fri 0800-1300, 1700-2000; Sat 0800-1300, although main offices in large towns will stay open all day. Stamps can be bought here or at *estancos* (tobacconists).

## Safety

Sevilla is a very safe place to travel. There's been a crackdown on tourist crime in recent years and Sevilla feels much safer than a city of equivalent size in England.

What tourist crime there is tends to be of the opportunistic kind. Robberies from parked cars (particularly those with foreign plates) or snatch-and-run thefts from vehicles stopped at traffic lights are not unknown, and the occasional mugger operates in Sevilla. Keep car doors locked when driving. If parking in Sevilla city or a popular hiking zone, make it clear there's nothing worth robbing in a car by opening the glove compartment.

If you are unfortunate enough to be robbed, you should report the theft immediately at the nearest police station, as insurance companies will require a copy of the *denuncia* (police report).

## Smoking

Smoking is widespread in Spain, but it's been banned in all enclosed public spaces (ie bars and restaurants) since 2011. There are still rooms for smokers in some hotels, but these are limited to 30% of the total rooms. Prices are standardized; you can buy cigarettes at tobacconists or at machines in cafés and bars (with a small surcharge).

## Student travellers

An **International Student Identity Card** (ISIC; www.isic.org), for full-time students, is worth having in Spain. Get one at your place of study, or at many travel agencies both in and outside Spain. The cost varies from country to country, but is generally about €6-10 – a good investment, providing discounts of up to 20% on some plane fares, train tickets, museum entries, bus tickets and some accommodation. A **European Youth Card** (www.eyca.org) card gives similar discounts for anyone under 30 years of age.

## Taxes

Nearly all goods and services in Spain are subject to a value-added tax (IVA). This is 10% for things like supermarket supplies, hotels and restaurant meals, but is 21% on luxury goods such as computer equipment. IVA is normally included in the stated prices. You're technically entitled to claim it back if you're a non-EU citizen, for purchases over €90. If you're buying something pricey, make sure you get a stamped receipt clearly showing the IVA component, as well as your name and passport number; you can claim the amount back at major airports on departure. Some shops will have a form to smooth the process.

## Telephone

**Country code** +34; **IDD Code** 00
Phone booths on the street are dwindling. Those that remain are mostly operated by **Telefónica**, and all have international direct dialling. They accept coins from €0.05 upwards and phone cards, which can be bought from *kioscos* (newspaper kiosks).

Domestic landlines have 9-digit numbers beginning with 9. Although the first 3 digits indicate the province, you have to dial the full number from wherever you are calling, including abroad. Mobile numbers start with 6.

Most foreign mobiles will work in Spain (although older North American ones won't); check with your service provider about what the call costs will be like. Roaming charges within the EU are set to be abolished from late 2015. Many mobile networks require you to call before leaving your home country to activate overseas service (roaming). If you're staying a while and have an unlocked phone, it's pretty cheap to buy a Spanish SIM card.

## Time

1 hr ahead of GMT. Clocks go forward an hour in late Mar and back in late Oct with the rest of the EU.

## Tipping

Tipping in Spain is far from compulsory. A 10% tip would be considered extremely generous in a restaurant; 3% to 5% is more usual. It's rare for a service charge to be added to a bill. Waiters don't expect tips but in bars and cafés people will sometimes leave small change, especially for table service. Taxi drivers don't expect a tip, but will be pleased to receive one.

## Tourist information

The tourist information infrastructure in Andalucía is organized by the Junta (the regional government) and is generally excellent, with a wide range of information, often in English, German and French as well as Spanish. The website www.andalucia.org has comprehensive information and *Oficinas de turismo* (local government tourist offices) are in all the major towns, providing more specific local information. In addition, many towns run a municipal *turismo*, offering locally produced material. The tourist offices are generally open during normal office hours and in the main holiday areas normally have enthusiastic, multilingual staff. The tourist offices can provide local maps and town plans and a full list of registered accommodation. Staff are not allowed to make recommendations. If you're in a car, it's especially worth asking for a listing of *casas rurales* (rural accommodation). In villages with no *turismo* you could try asking for local information on accommodation and sights in the *ayuntamiento* (town hall).

There is a substantial amount of tourist information on the internet. Apart from the websites listed (see below), many towns and villages have their own site with information on sights, hotels and restaurants, although this may be in Spanish.

The **Spanish Tourist Board** (www. spain.info) produces a mass of information that you can obtain before you leave from their offices located in many countries abroad.

## Useful websites

**www.alsa.es** One of the country's main bus companies with online booking.

**www.andalucia.com** Excellent site with comprehensive practical and background information on Andalucía, covering everything from accommodation to zoos.

**www.andalucia.org** The official tourist-board site, with details of even the smallest villages, accommodation and tourist offices.

**www.booking.com** The most useful online accommodation booker for Spain.

**www.dgt.es** The transport department website has up-to-date information in Spanish on road conditions throughout the country.

**www.elpais.com** Online edition of Spain's biggest-selling daily paper. Also in English.

**www.guiarepsol.com** Online route planner for Spanish roads, also available in English.

**www.inm.es** Site of the national metereological institute, with the day's weather and next-day forecasts.

**www.inturjoven.com** Details of youth hostel locations, facilities and prices.

**maps.google.es** Street maps of most Spanish towns and cities.

**www.movelia.es** Online timetables and ticketing for some bus companies.

**www.paginasamarillas.es** Yellow Pages.

**www.paginasblancas.es** White Pages.

**www.parador.es** Parador information, including locations, prices and photos.

**www.raar.es** Andalucían rural accommodation network with details of mainly self-catering accommodation to rent, including cottages and farmhouses.

**www.renfe.com** Online timetables and tickets for RENFE train network.

**www.spain.info** The official website of the Spanish tourist board.

**www.soccer-spain.com** A website in English dedicated to Spanish football.

**www.ticketmaster.es** Spain's biggest ticketing agency for concerts and more, with online purchase.

**www.toprural.com** and **www.todo turismorural.com** 2 of many sites for *casas rurales*.

**www.tourspain.es** A useful website run by the Spanish tourist board.

**www.typicallyspanish.com** News and links on all things Spanish.

## Tour operators

### UK and Ireland

**Abercrombie and Kent**, www.abercrombiekent.com. Upmarket operator offering tailor-made itineraries in Andalucía as well as the rest of Spain.

**ACE Cultural Tours**, www.aceculturaltours.co.uk. Trips focusing on Moorish culture, as well as wildlife.

**Andante Travels**, www.andantetravels.com. Popular operator running a variety of different cultural and active holidays in Andalucía. They focus on archaeology and the Roman presence.

**Cycling Safaris**, www.cyclingsafaris.com. Irish operator offering well-priced tours to Andalucía.

**Exodus**, www.exodus.co.uk. Walking and adventure tours to suit all pockets.

**Martin Randall Travel**, www.martinrandall.com. Excellent cultural itineraries accompanied by lectures. Covers all the main cities, and also has an off-beat tour visiting some out-of-the-way spots.

### Rest of Europe
**Bravo Bike Travel**, www.bravobike.com. Runs 8-day bike tours of Andalucía.

### North America
**Cycling Through The Centuries**, www.cycling-centuries.com. Runs guided cycling tours of Andalucía.
**Epiculinary Tours**, www.epiculinary. com. Tours to delight foodies, with lessons on making tapas and other Andalucían food interspersed with plenty of tastings and cultural visits.
**Heritage Tours**, www.htprivatetravel. com. Interesting, classy itineraries around the south of Spain.
**Magical Spain**, www.magicalspain.com. American-run tour agency based in Sevilla, who runs a variety of tours.
**Spain Adventures**, www.spain adventures.com. Organizes a range of hiking and biking tours.

### Australia
**Ibertours**,www.ibertours.com.au. Spanish specialist and booking agent for **Parador** and **Rusticae** hotels.
**Timeless Tours & Travel**, www.timeless. com.au. Specializes in tailored itineraries for Spain.

## Visas and immigration

EU citizens and those from countries within the Schengen agreement can enter Spain freely. UK and Irish citizens will need to carry a passport, while an identity card suffices for other EU/Schengen nationals. Citizens of Australia, the USA, Canada, New Zealand, several Latin American countries and Israel can enter without a visa for up to 90 days. Other citizens will require a visa, obtainable from Spanish consulates or embassies. These are usually issued quickly and are valid for all Schengen countries. The basic visa is valid for 90 days, and you'll need 2 passport photos, proof of funds covering your stay, and possibly evidence of medical cover (ie insurance).

For extensions of visas, apply to an *oficina de extranjeros* in a major city (usually in the *comisaría*, main police station).

## Weights and measures

Metric.

## Women travellers

While there's still the odd wolf-whistling dinosaur lurking around Andalucía, female travellers shouldn't encounter any harassment at all.

## Working in the country

The most obvious paid work for English speakers is through teaching the language. Even the smallest towns usually have an English college or two. Rates of pay aren't great except in the large cities, but you can live quite comfortably. The best way of finding work is by trawling around the schools, but there are dozens of useful internet sites; check www.eslcafe.com for links and listings. There's also a more casual scene of private teaching; noticeboards in universities and student cafés are the best way to find work of this sort, or to advertise your own services. Standard rates for 1-to-1 classes are €15-30 per hr.

Bar work is also relatively easy to find, particularly in summer on the coast. Live-in English-speaking au pairs and childminders are also popular with wealthier city families. The **International Au Pair Association** (www.iapa.org) lists reliable agencies that arrange placements. The online forum **Au Pair World** (www.aupairworld.net) is a popular free service.

EU citizens are at an advantage when it comes to working in Spain; they can work without a permit. Non-EU citizens need a working visa, obtainable from Spanish embassies or consulates, but you'll need to have a firm offer of work to obtain it. Most English schools can organize this for you but make sure you arrange it before arriving in the country.

# Basic Spanish

Learning Spanish is a useful part of the preparation for a trip to Spain and no volumes of dictionaries, phrase books or word lists will provide the same enjoyment as being able to communicate directly with the people of the country you are visiting. It is a good idea to make an effort to grasp the basics before you go. As you travel you will pick up more of the language and the more you know, the more you will benefit from your stay. Regional accents and usages vary, but the basic language is essentially the same everywhere.

## Vowels

| | |
|---|---|
| *a* | as in English *cat* |
| *e* | as in English *best* |
| *i* | as the ee in English *feet* |
| *o* | as in English *shop* |
| *u* | as the oo in English *food* |
| *ai* | as the i in English *ride* |
| *ei* | as ey in English *they* |
| *oi* | as oy in English *toy* |

## Consonants

Most consonants can be pronounced more or less as they are in English. The exceptions are:

| | |
|---|---|
| *g* | before *e* or *i* is the same as *j* |
| *h* | is always silent (except in *ch* as in *chair*) |
| *j* | as the *ch* in Scottish *loch* |
| *ll* | as the *y* in *yellow* |
| *ñ* | as the *ni* in English *onion* |
| *rr* | trilled much more than in English |
| *x* | depending on its location, pronounced *x*, *s*, *sh* or *j* |

## Spanish words and phrases

### Greetings, courtesies

| | | | |
|---|---|---|---|
| hello | *hola* | thank you (very much) | *(muchas) gracias* |
| good morning | *buenos días* | | |
| good afternoon/evening | *buenas tardes/ noches* | I speak a little Spanish | *hablo un poco de español* |
| goodbye | *adiós/ hasta luego* | I don't speak Spanish | *no hablo español* |
| | | do you speak English? | *¿hablas inglés?* |
| pleased to meet you | *encantado/a* | I don't understand | *no entiendo* |
| how are you? | *¿cómo estás?* | please speak slowly | *habla despacio por favor* |
| I'm called ... | *me llamo ...* | | |
| what is your name? | *¿cómo te llamas?* | I am very sorry | *lo siento mucho/ discúlpame* |
| I'm fine, thanks | *muy bien, gracias* | what do you want? | *¿qué quieres?* |
| | | I want/would like | *quiero/quería* |
| yes/no | *sí/no* | I don't want it | *no lo quiero* |
| please | *por favor* | good/bad | *bueno/malo* |

## Basic questions and requests

| | | | |
|---|---|---|---|
| have you got a room for two people? | | when? | *¿cuándo?* |
| *¿tienes una habitación para dos personas?* | | where is_? | *¿dónde está_?* |
| | | where can I buy? | *¿dónde puedo comprar...?* |
| how do I get to_? | *¿cómo llego a_?* | | |
| how much does it cost? | | where is the nearest petrol station? | |
| *¿cuánto cuesta? ¿cuánto es?* | | *¿dónde está la gasolinera más cercana?* | |
| is VAT included? | *¿el IVA está incluido?* | why? | *¿por qué?* |
| when does the bus leave (arrive)? | | | |
| *¿a qué hora sale (llega) el autobús?* | | | |

## Basic words and phrases

| | | | |
|---|---|---|---|
| bank | *el banco* | market | *el mercado* |
| bathroom/toilet | *el baño* | note/coin | *el billete/la moneda* |
| to be | *ser, estar* | police (policeman) | *la policía (el policía)* |
| bill | *la factura/la cuenta* | post office | *el correo* |
| cash | *efectivo* | public telephone | *el teléfono público* |
| cheap | *barato/a* | shop | *la tienda* |
| credit card | *la tarjeta de crédito* | supermarket | *el supermercado* |
| exchange rate | *el tipo de cambio* | there is/are | *hay* |
| expensive | *caro/a* | there isn't/aren't | *no hay* |
| to go | *ir* | ticket office | *la taquilla* |
| to have | *tener, haber* | traveller's cheques | *los cheques de viaje* |

## Getting around

| | | | |
|---|---|---|---|
| aeroplane | *el avión* | luggage | *el equipaje* |
| airport | *el aeropuerto* | motorway, freeway | *el autopista/autovía* |
| arrival/departure | *la llegada/salida* | north/south/ | *el norte, el sur,* |
| avenue | *la avenida* | west/east | *el oeste, el este* |
| border | *la frontera* | oil | *el aceite* |
| bus station | *la estación de autobuses* | to park | *aparcar* |
| | | passport | *el pasaporte* |
| bus | *el bus/el autobús/ el camión* | petrol/gasoline | *la gasolina* |
| | | puncture | *el pinchazo* |
| corner | *la esquina* | street | *la calle* |
| customs | *la aduana* | that way | *por allí* |
| left/right | *izquierda/derecha* | this way | *por aquí* |
| ticket | *el billete* | tyre | *el neumático* |
| empty/full | *vacío/lleno* | unleaded | *sin plomo* |
| highway, main road | *la carretera* | waiting room | *la sala de espera* |
| insurance | *el seguro* | to walk | *caminar/andar* |
| insured person | *el asegurado/la asegurada* | | |

## Accommodation

| | | | |
|---|---|---|---|
| air conditioning | el aire acondicionado | restaurant | el restaurante |
| all-inclusive | todo incluido | room/bedroom | la habitación |
| bathroom, private | el baño privado | sheets | las sábanas |
| bed, double | la cama matrimonial | shower | la ducha |
| blankets | las mantas | soap | el jabón |
| to clean | limpiar | toilet | el inódoro |
| dining room | el comedor | toilet paper | el papel higiénico |
| hotel | el hotel | towels, clean/dirty | las toallas limpias sucias |
| noisy | ruidoso | water, hot/cold | el agua caliente/ fría |
| pillows | las almohadas | | |

## Health

| | | | |
|---|---|---|---|
| aspirin | la aspirina | diarrhoea | la diarrea |
| blood | la sangre | doctor | el médico |
| chemist | la farmacia | fever/sweat | la fiebre/el sudor |
| condoms | los preservativos, los condones | pain | el dolor |
| | | head | la cabeza |
| contact lenses | los lentes de contacto | period | la regla |
| | | sanitary towels | las toallas femininas |
| contraceptives | los anticonceptivos | stomach | el estómago |
| contraceptive pill | la píldora anticonceptiva | | |

## Family

| | | | |
|---|---|---|---|
| family | la familia | boyfriend/girlfriend | el novio/la novia |
| brother/sister | el hermano/ la hermana | friend | el amigo/ la amiga |
| daughter/son | la hija/el hijo | married | casado/a |
| father/mother | el padre/la madre | single/unmarried | soltero/a |
| husband/wife | el esposo (marido)/la mujer | | |

## Months, days and time

| | | | |
|---|---|---|---|
| January | enero | July | julio |
| February | febrero | August | agosto |
| March | marzo | September | septiembre |
| April | abril | October | octubre |
| May | mayo | November | noviembre |
| June | junio | December | diciembre |

| | | | |
|---|---|---|---|
| Monday | *lunes* | it's one o'clock | *es la una* |
| Tuesday | *martes* | it's seven o'clock | *son las siete* |
| Wednesday | *miércoles* | it's six twenty | *son las seis y veinte* |
| Thursday | *jueves* | | |
| Friday | *viernes* | it's five to nine | *son las nueve menos cinco* |
| Saturday | *sábado* | | |
| Sunday | *domingo* | in ten minutes | *en diez minutos* |
| at one o'clock | *a la una* | five hours | *cinco horas* |
| at half past two | *a las dos y media* | does it take long? | *¿tarda mucho?* |
| at a quarter to three | *a las tres menos cuarto* | | |

### Numbers

| | | | |
|---|---|---|---|
| one | *uno* | sixteen | *dieciséis* |
| two | *dos* | seventeen | *diecisiete* |
| three | *tres* | eighteen | *dieciocho* |
| four | *cuatro* | nineteen | *diecinueve* |
| five | *cinco* | twenty | *veinte* |
| six | *seis* | twenty-one | *veintiuno* |
| seven | *siete* | thirty | *treinta* |
| eight | *ocho* | forty | *cuarenta* |
| nine | *nueve* | fifty | *cincuenta* |
| ten | *diez* | sixty | *sesenta* |
| eleven | *once* | seventy | *setenta* |
| twelve | *doce* | eighty | *ochenta* |
| thirteen | *trece* | ninety | *noventa* |
| fourteen | *catorce* | hundred | *cien/ciento* |
| fifteen | *quince* | thousand | *mil* |

# Food glossary

**A**

| | |
|---|---|
| acedía | small wedge sole |
| aceite | oil; *aceite de oliva* is olive oil and *aceite de girasol* is sunflower oil |
| aceitunas | olives, also sometimes called *olivas*. The best kind are unripe green *manzanilla*, particularly when stuffed with anchovy, *rellenas con anchoas* |
| adobo | marinated fried nuggets usually of shark (*tiburón*) or dogfish (*cazón*); delicious |
| agua | water |
| aguacate | avocado |
| ahumado | smoked; *tabla de ahumados* is a mixed plate of smoked fish |
| ajillo (al) | cooked in garlic, most commonly *gambas* or *pollo* |
| ajo | garlic, *ajetes* are young garlic shoots, often in a *revuelto* |
| ajo arriero | a simple sauce of garlic, paprika and parsley |
| ajo blanco | a chilled garlic and almond soup, a speciality of Málaga |
| albóndigas | meatballs |
| alcachofa/ alcaucil | artichoke |
| alcaparras | capers |
| aliño | any salad marinated in vinegar, olive oil and salt; often made with egg or potato, with chopped onion, peppers and tomato |
| alioli | a tasty sauce made from raw garlic blended with oil and egg yolk; also called *ajoaceite* |
| almejas | name applied to various species of small clams, often cooked with garlic, parsley and white wine |
| almendra | almond |
| alubias | broad beans |
| anchoa | preserved anchovy |
| anchoba/ anjova | bluefish |
| añejo | aged (of cheeses, rums, etc) |
| angulas | baby eels, a delicacy that has become scarce and expensive. Far more common are *gulas*, false *angulas* made from putting processed fish through a spaghetti machine; squid ink is used for authentic colouring |
| anís | aniseed, commonly used to flavour biscuits and liqueurs |
| arroz | rice; *arroz con leche* is a sweet rice pudding |
| asado | roast. An *asador* is a restaurant specializing in charcoal-roasted meat and fish |
| atún | blue-fin tuna |
| azúcar | sugar |

## B

| | |
|---|---|
| bacalao | salted cod, either superb or leathery |
| berberechos | cockles |
| berenjena | aubergine/eggplant |
| besugo | red bream |
| bistec | steak. *Poco hecho* is rare, *al punto* is medium rare, *regular* is medium, *muy hecho* is well done |
| bizcocho | sponge cake or biscuit |
| bocadillo/ bocata | a crusty filled roll |
| bogavante | lobster |
| bonito | atlantic bonito, a small tuna fish |
| boquerones | fresh anchovies, often served filleted in garlic and oil |
| botella | bottle |
| (a la) brasa | cooked on a griddle over coals |
| buey | ox |

## C

| | |
|---|---|
| caballa | mackerel |
| cacahuetes | peanuts |
| café | coffee; *solo* is black, served espresso-style; *cortado* adds a dash of milk, *con leche* more; *americano* is a long black coffee |
| calamares | squid |
| caldereta | a stew of meat or fish usually made with sherry; *venao* (venison) is commonly used, and delicious |
| caldo | a thin soup |
| callos | tripe |
| caña | a glass of draught beer |
| cangrejo | crab; occasionally river crayfish |

| | |
|---|---|
| caracol | snail; very popular in Sevilla *cabrillas*, *burgaos*, and *blanquillos* are popular varieties |
| caramelos | boiled sweets |
| carne | meat |
| carta | menu |
| casero | home-made |
| castañas | chestnuts |
| cava | sparkling wine, mostly produced in Catalunya |
| cazuela | a stew, often of fish or seafood |
| cebolla | onion |
| cena | dinner |
| centollo | spider crab |
| cerdo | pork |
| cerezas | cherries |
| cerveza | beer |
| champiñón | mushroom |
| chipirones | small squid, often served *en su tinta*, in its own ink, mixed with butter and garlic |
| chocolate | a popular afternoon drink; also slang for hashish |
| choco | cuttlefish |
| chorizo | a red sausage, versatile and of varying spiciness (*picante*) |
| choto | roast kid |
| chuleta/ chuletilla | chop |
| chuletón | a massive T-bone steak, often sold by weight |
| churrasco | barbecued meat, often ribs with a spicy sauce |
| churro | a fried dough-stick usually eaten with hot chocolate (*chocolate con churros*). Usually eaten as a late afternoon snack (*merienda*), but sometimes for breakfast |

| | |
|---|---|
| cigala | Dublin Bay prawn/Norway lobster |
| ciruela | plum |
| cochinillo | suckling pig |
| cocido | a heavy stew, usually of meat and chickpeas/beans; *sopa de cocido* is the broth |
| codorniz | quail |
| cogollo | lettuce heart |
| comida | lunch |
| conejo | rabbit |
| congrio | conger eel |
| cordero | lamb |
| costillas | ribs |
| crema catalana | a lemony crème brûlée |
| criadillas | hog or bull testicles |
| croquetas | deep-fried crumbed balls of meat, béchamel, seafood, or vegetables |
| cuchara | spoon |
| cuchillo | knife |
| cuenta (la) | the bill |

## D

| | |
|---|---|
| desayuno | breakfast |
| dorada | a species of bream (gilthead) |
| dulce | sweet |

## E

| | |
|---|---|
| ecológico | organic |
| embutido | any salami-type sausage |
| empanada | a pie, pasty-like (*empanadilla*) or in large flat tins and sold by the slice; *atun* or *bonito* is a common filling, as is ham, mince or seafood |
| ensalada | salad; *mixta* is usually a large serve of a bit of everything; excellent option |
| ensaladilla rusa | Russian salad, with potato, peas and carrots in mayonnaise |
| escabeche | pickled in wine and vinegar |
| espárragos | asparagus, white and usually canned |
| espinacas | spinach |
| estofado | braised, often in stew form |

## F

| | |
|---|---|
| fabada | the most famous of Asturian dishes, a hearty stew of beans, *chorizo*, and *morcilla* |
| fideuá | a bit like a paella but with noodles |
| filete | steak |
| fino | the classic dry sherry |
| flamenquín | a fried and crumbed finger of meat stuffed with ham |
| flan | the ubiquitous crème caramel, great when home-made (*casero*), awful when it's not |
| foie | fattened goose liver; often made into a thick gravy sauce |
| frambuesas | raspberries |
| fresas | strawberries |
| frito/a | fried |
| fruta | fruit |

## G

| | |
|---|---|
| galletas | biscuits |
| gallo | rooster, also the flatfish megrim |
| gambas | prawns |
| garbanzos | chickpeas, often served in *espinacas con garbanzos*, a spicy spinach dish that is a signature of Seville |
| gazpacho | a cold garlicky tomato soup, very refreshing |

| | |
|---|---|
| granizado | popular summer drink, like a frappé fruit milkshake |
| guisado/ guiso | stewed/a stew |
| guisantes | peas |

## H

| | |
|---|---|
| habas | broad beans, often deliciously stewed *con jamón*, with ham |
| harina | flour |
| helado | ice cream |
| hígado | liver |
| higo | fig |
| hojaldre | puff pastry |
| horno (al) | oven (baked) |
| hueva | fish roe |
| huevo | egg |

## I/J

| | |
|---|---|
| ibérico | see *jamón*; the term can also refer to other pork products |
| infusión | herbal tea |
| jabalí | wild boar |
| jamón | ham; *jamón York* is cooked British-style ham. Far better is cured *jamón serrano*; *ibérico* ham comes from Iberian pigs in western Spain fed on acorns (*bellotas*). Some places, like Jabugo, are famous for their hams, which can be expensive |
| judías verdes | green beans |
| jerez (al) | cooked in sherry |

## L

| | |
|---|---|
| langosta | crayfish |
| langostinos | king prawns |
| lechazo | milk-fed lamb |
| leche | milk |

| | |
|---|---|
| lechuga | lettuce |
| lengua | tongue |
| lenguado | sole |
| lentejas | lentils |
| limón | lemon |
| lomo | loin, usually sliced pork, sometimes tuna |
| lubina | sea bass |

## M

| | |
|---|---|
| macedonia de frutas | fruit salad, usually tinned |
| manchego | Spain's national cheese; hard, whitish and made from ewe's milk |
| manitas (de cerdo) | pork trotters |
| mantequilla | butter |
| manzana | apple |
| manzanilla | the dry, salty sherry from Sanlúcar de Barrameda; also, confusingly, camomile tea and the tastiest type of olive |
| marisco | shellfish |
| mejillones | mussels |
| melocotón | peach, usually canned and served in *almíbar* (syrup) |
| melva | frigate mackerel, often served tinned or semi-dried |
| menestra | a vegetable stew, usually served like a minestrone without the liquid; vegetarians will be annoyed to find that it's often seeded with ham and bits of pork |
| menú | a set meal, usually consisting of three or more courses, bread and wine or water |

| | |
|---|---|
| menudo | tripe stew, usually with chickpeas and mint |
| merluza | hake is to Spain as rice is to southeast Asia |
| mero | grouper |
| miel | honey |
| migas | breadcrumbs, fried and often mixed with lard and meat to form a delicious rural dish of the same name |
| Mojama | salt-cured tuna, most common in Cádiz province |
| mollejas | sweetbreads; ie the pancreas of a calf or lamb |
| montadito | a small toasted filled roll |
| morcilla | blood sausage, either solid or semi-liquid |
| morro | cheek, pork or lamb |
| mostaza | mustard |
| mosto | grape juice. Can also refer to a young wine, from 3 months old |

## N

| | |
|---|---|
| naranja | orange |
| nata | sweet whipped cream |
| natillas | rich custard dessert |
| navajas | razor shells |
| nécora | small sea crab, sometimes called a velvet crab |
| nueces | walnuts |

## O

| | |
|---|---|
| orejas | ears, usually of a pig |
| orujo | a fiery grape spirit, often brought to add to black coffee if the waiter likes you |
| ostras | oysters, also a common expression of dismay |

## P

| | |
|---|---|
| paella | rice dish with saffron, seafood and/or meat |
| pan | bread |
| parrilla | grill; a *parrillada* is a mixed grill |
| pastel | cake/pastry |
| patatas | potatoes; often chips (*patatas fritas*, which confusingly can also refer to crisps); *bravas* are with a spicy tomato sauce |
| pato | duck |
| pavía | a crumbed and fried nugget of fish, usually *bacalao* or *merluza* |
| pavo | turkey |
| pechuga | breast (usually chicken) |
| perdiz | partridge |
| pescado | fish |
| pescaíto frito | Andalucían deep-fried fish and seafood |
| pestiños | an Arabic-style confection of pastry and honey, traditionally eaten during Semana Santa |
| pez espada | swordfish; delicious; sometimes called *emperador* |
| picadillo | a dish of spicy mincemeat |
| picante | hot, ie spicy |
| pichón | squab |
| pijota | whiting |
| pimienta | pepper |
| pimientos | peppers; there are many kinds, *piquillos* are the trademark thin Basque red pepper; Padrón produces sweet green mini ones. A popular tapa is *pimientos aliñados* (marinated roasted peppers, often with onion, sometimes with tuna) |

| | | | |
|---|---|---|---|
| **pincho** | a small snack or grilled meat on a skewer (or *pinchito*) | **raya** | any of a variety of rays and skates |
| **pipas** | sunflower seeds, a common snack | **rebujito** | a weak mix of *manzanilla* and lemonade, consumed by the bucketload during Andalucían festivals |
| **pisto** | a ratatouille-like vegetable concoction | | |
| **plancha (a la)** | grilled on a hot iron or fried in a pan without oil | **relleno/a** | stuffed |
| **plátano** | banana | **reserva, gran reserva, crianza** | terms relating to the age of wines; *gran reserva* is the oldest and finest, then *reserva* followed by *crianza* |
| **pluma** | a cut of pork next to the loin | | |
| **pollo** | chicken | | |
| **postre** | dessert | | |
| **potaje** | a soup or stew | **revuelto** | scrambled eggs, usually with wild mushrooms (*setas*) or seafood; often a speciality |
| **pringá** | a tasty paste of stewed meats usually eaten in a *montadito* and a traditional final tapa of the evening | | |
| | | **riñones** | kidneys |
| **puerros** | leeks | **rodaballo** | turbot; pricey and delicious |
| **pulpo** | octopus, particularly delicious *a la gallega*, boiled Galician style and garnished with olive oil, salt and paprika | **romana (à la)** | fried in batter |
| | | **rosca** | a large round dish, a cross between sandwich and pizza |
| **puntillitas** | small squid, often served crumbed and deep fried | **rosquilla** | doughnut |

## Q/R

| | |
|---|---|
| **queso** | cheese; *de cabra* (goat's), *oveja* (sheep's) or *vaca* (cow's). It comes fresh (*fresco*), medium (*semi-curado*) or strong (*curado*) |
| **rabo de buey/toro** | oxtail |
| **ración** | a portion of food served in cafés and bars; check the size and order a half (*media*) if you want less |
| **rana** | frog; *ancas de rana* is frogs' legs |
| **rape** | monkfish/anglerfish |

## S

| | |
|---|---|
| **sal** | salt |
| **salchicha** | sausage |
| **salchichón** | a salami-like sausage |
| **salmón** | salmon |
| **salmonete** | red mullet |
| **salmorejo** | a delicious thicker version of gazpacho, often garnished with egg and cured ham |
| **salpicón** | a seafood salad with plenty of onion and vinegar |
| **salsa** | sauce |
| **San Jacobo** | a steak cooked with ham and cheese |
| **sandía** | watermelon |
| **sardinas** | sardines, delicious grilled |

| | |
|---|---|
| **sargo** | white sea bream |
| **seco** | dry |
| **secreto** | a cut of pork loin |
| **sepia** | cuttlefish |
| **serrano** | see *jamón* |
| **setas** | wild mushrooms, often superb |
| **sidra** | cider |
| **solomillo** | beef or pork steak cut from the sirloin bone, deliciously fried in whisky and garlic in Sevilla (*solomillo al whisky*) |
| **sopa** | soup; *sopa castellana* is a broth with a fried egg, noodles, and bits of ham |

## T

| | |
|---|---|
| **tapa** | a saucer-sized portion of bar food |
| **tarta** | tart or cake |
| **té** | tea |
| **tenedor** | fork |
| **ternera** | veal or young beef |
| **tinto** | red wine is *vino tinto*; a *tinto de verano* is mixed with lemonade and ice, a refreshing option |
| **tocino** | pork lard; *tocinillo de cielo* is a caramelized egg dessert |

| | |
|---|---|
| **tomate** | tomato |
| **torrijas** | a Semana Santa dessert, bread fried in milk and covered in honey and cinnamon |
| **tortilla** | a Spanish omelette, with potato, egg, olive oil and optional onion; *tortilla francesa* is a French omelette |
| **tostada** | toasted, also a toasted breakfast roll eaten with olive oil, tomato or pâté |
| **trucha** | trout |

## U/V

| | |
|---|---|
| **uva** | grape |
| **vaso** | glass |
| **venado/ venao** | venison |
| **verduras** | vegetables |
| **vieiras** | scallops, also called *veneras* |
| **vino** | wine; *blanco* is white, *rosado* or *clarete* is rosé, *tinto* is red |

## Z

| | |
|---|---|
| **zanahoria** | carrot |
| **zumo** | fruit juice, usually bottled and pricey |

# Glossary of architectural terms

## A

**alcázar**   a Moorish fort

**ambulatory**   a gallery round the chancel and behind the altar

**apse**   vaulted square or rounded recess at the back of a church

**archivolt**   decorative carving around the outer surface of an arch

**art deco**   a style that evolved between the World Wars, based on geometric forms

**artesonado ceiling**   ceiling of carved wooden panels with Islamic motifs popular throughout Spain in the 15th and 16th centuries

**ayuntamiento**   a town hall

**azulejo**   an ornamental ceramic tile

## B

**Baldacchino**   an ornate carved canopy above an altar or tomb

**Baroque**   ornate architectural style of the 17th and 18th centuries

**bodega**   a cellar where wine is kept or made; the term also refers to modern wineries and wine shops

**buttress**   a pillar built into a wall to reinforce areas of greatest stress. A flying buttress is set away from the wall; a feature of Gothic architecture

## C

**capilla**   a chapel within a church or cathedral

**capital**   the top of column, joining it to another section. Often highly decorated

**castillo**   a castle or fort

**catedral**   a cathedral, ie the seat of a bishop

**chancel**   the area of a church which contains the main altar, usually at the eastern end

**chapterhouse**   area reserved for Bible study in monastery or church

**Churrigueresque**   a particularly ornate form of Spanish Baroque, named after the Churriguera brothers

**colegiata**   a collegiate church, ie one ruled by a chapter of canons

**conjunto histórico**   a tourist-board term referring to an area of historic buildings

| | | | |
|---|---|---|---|
| convento | a monastery or convent | **M** | |
| coro | the area enclosing the choirstalls, often central and completely closed off in Spanish churches | mocárabes | small concave spaces used as a decorative feature on Moorish ceilings and archways |
| crossing | the centre of a church, where the 'arms' of the cross join | modernista | a particularly imaginative variant of art nouveau that came out of Catalonia; exemplified by Gaudí |
| **E** | | monasterio | a large monastery usually located in a rural area |
| ermita | a hermitage or rural chapel | monstrance | a ceremonial container for displaying the host |
| **G** | | Mozarabic | the style of Christian artisans living under Moorish rule |
| Gothic | 13th-15th-century style formerly known as pointed style; distinguished externally by pinnacles and tracery around windows, Gothic architecture lays stress on the presence of light | mudéjar | the work of Muslims living under Christian rule after the Reconquest, characterized by ornate brickwork |
| | | multifoil | a type of Muslim-influenced arch with consecutive circular depressions |
| **H** | | muralla | a city wall |
| hospital | in pilgrimage terms, a place where pilgrims used to be able to rest, receive nourishment and receive medical attention | **N** | |
| | | nave | the main body of the church, a single or multiple passageway leading (usually) from the western end up to the crossing or high altar |
| **I** | | | |
| iglesia | a church | | |
| **L** | | neoclassical | a reaction against the excesses of Spanish Baroque, this 18th- and 19th-century style saw clean lines and symmetry valued above all things |
| lobed arch | Moorish arch with depressions in the shape of simple arches | | |
| lonja | a guildhall or fish market | | |

## P

**palacio**  a palace or large residence

**patio**  an interior courtyard

**pediment**  triangular section between top of collums and gables

**pilaster**  pillar attached to the wall

**Plateresque**  derived from *platero* (silversmith); used to describe a Spanish Renaissance style characterized by finely carved decoration

## R

**reliquary**  a container to hold bones or remains of saints and other holy things

**Renaissance**  Spanish Renaissance architecture began when classical motifs were used in combination with Gothic elements in the 16th century

**retablo**  altarpiece or retable formed by many panels often rising to roof level; can be painted or sculptured

**Romanesque (románico)**  style spread from France in the 11th and 12th centuries, characterized by barrel vaulting, rounded apses and semicircular arches

**Romano**  Roman

## S

**sacristy (sacristía)**  part of church reserved for priests to prepare for services

**soportales**  wooden or stone supports for the 1st floor of civic buildings, forming an arcade underneath

**stucco (yesería)**  moulding mix consisting mainly of plaster; fundamental part of Moorish architecture

# Index → *Entries in* **bold** *refer to maps*

## FOOTPRINT
### Features

# Credits

**Footprint credits**
**Editor**: Jo Williams
**Production and layout**: Emma Bryers
**Maps**: Kevin Feeney
**Colour section**: Angus Dawson

**Publisher**: Patrick Dawson
**Managing Editor**: Felicity Laughton
**Administration**: Elizabeth Taylor
**Advertising sales and marketing**:
John Sadler, Kirsty Holmes

**Photography credits**
**Front cover**: Dome in the Real Alcázar
Copyright: Antonio Jodice/
Dreamstime.com
**Back cover top**: Plaza de España
Copyright: Javarman/Dreamstime.com
**Back cover bottom**: Patio in the
Real Alcázar
Copyright: Renata Sedmakova/
Shutterstock.com

**Colour section**
**Inside front cover**: superstock: Alvaro
Leiva/age fotostock, Travel Library Limited/
Travel Library Limited, Felipe Rodríguez/age
fotostock. **Page 1**: superstock: age fotostock/
age fotostock. **Page 2**: superstock: Cusp/Cusp.
**Page 4**: shutterstock: Barone Firenze;
superstock: Lucas Vallecillos/age fotostock, age
fotostock/age fotostock. **Page 5**: superstock:
Hemis.fr/Hemis.fr, Tibor Bognár/age fotostock,
Travel Library Limited/Travel Library Limited,
Album/Oronoz /Album, . **Page 7**: shutterstock:
Aleksandar Todorovic, monysasu; superstock:
Frischknecht Patrick/Prisma. **Page 8**:
superstock: age fotostock/age fotostock.

Printed in Spain by GraphyCem

The content of *Seville 2nd edition* has
been taken directly from Footprint's
*Andalucía Handbook 8th edition*.

**Publishing information**
Footprint Seville
2nd edition
© Footprint Handbooks Ltd
April 2015

ISBN: 978 1 910120 25 5
CIP DATA: A catalogue record for this
book is available from the British Library

® Footprint Handbooks and the
Footprint mark are a registered
trademark of Footprint Handbooks Ltd

Published by Footprint
6 Riverside Court
Lower Bristol Road
Bath BA2 3DZ, UK
T +44 (0)1225 469141
F +44 (0)1225 469461
footprinttravelguides.com

Distributed in the USA by
National Book Network, Inc.

Every effort has been made to ensure
that the facts in this guidebook are
accurate. However, travellers should still
obtain advice from consulates, airlines,
etc about travel and visa requirements
before travelling. The authors and
publishers cannot accept responsibility
for any loss, injury or inconvenience
however caused.

All rights reserved. No part of this
publication may be reproduced, stored
in a retrieval system, or transmitted, in
any form or by any means, electronic,
mechanical, photocopying, recording,
or otherwise without the prior
permission of Footprint Handbooks Ltd.

# Join us online...

Follow **@FootprintBooks** on Twitter, like **Footprint Books** on **Facebook** and talk travel with us! Ask us questions, speak to our authors, swap stories and be kept up-to-date with travel news, exclusive discounts and fantastic competitions.

Upload your travel pics to our **Flickr** site and inspire others on where to go next.

And don't forget to visit us at        **footprint**travelguides.com

**Andy Symington**

Andy hails from Australia but has spent this millennium living in Spain, where the art, architecture, wilderness, people, and, let's face it, the food and wine, continue to inspire him.

Andy is an experienced travel writer and has authored several other Footprint guides including *Northern Spain* and several guides in the Focus series.

## Price codes

| Where to stay | |
|---|---|
| €€€€ | over €170 |
| €€€ | €110-170 |
| €€ | €60-110 |
| € | under €60 |

A standard double/twin room in high season.

| Restaurants | |
|---|---|
| €€€ | over €30 |
| €€ | €15-30 |
| € | under €15 |

A two-course meal (or two average *raciones*) for one person, without drinks.